TRIO
LISTENING
AND SPEAKING 3

The Intersection of
Vocabulary, Listening, & Speaking

Daniel Hamlin

OXFORD
UNIVERSITY PRESS

OXFORD
UNIVERSITY PRESS

198 Madison Avenue
New York, NY 10016 USA

Great Clarendon Street, Oxford, OX2 6DP, United Kingdom

Oxford University Press is a department of the University of Oxford.
It furthers the University's objective of excellence in research, scholarship,
and education by publishing worldwide. Oxford is a registered trade
mark of Oxford University Press in the UK and in certain other countries

ISBN: 978 0 19 420308 1 STUDENT BOOK 3 WITH ONLINE PRACTICE PACK
ISBN: 978 0 19 420305 0 STUDENT BOOK 3 AS PACK COMPONENT
ISBN: 978 0 19 420323 4 ONLINE PRACTICE WEBSITE

Printed in China

This book is printed on paper from certified and well-managed sources

ACKNOWLEDGEMENTS

Cover Design: Yin Ling Wong

Illustrations by: Ben Hasler, p.60 and 125; Joe Taylor, p.22 and 110.

*The publishers would like to thank the following for their kind permission to reproduce
photographs:* p.1 SuperStock, Yuri Arcurs Media/Superstock, Pressmaster/
Shutterstock; p.2 Hiya Images/Corbis/Getty Images, Shutterstock/Bloomua,
Rob Melnychuk/Getty Images; p.3 Paul Burns/Getty Images, Hero Images
Inc./Alamy Stock Photo, Michaelpuche/Shutterstock.com, Andresr/
Shutterstock, Tom Craig/Alamy Stock Photo, Michael A. Keller/Masterfile,
Jacek Chabraszewski/Shutterstock, Gaspar Janos/Shutterstock, Russ Ensley/
Alamy Stock Photo; p.4 Shutterstock/Brocreative, Dennis MacDonald/Getty
Images, Visionsi/Shutterstock, Ron Chapple Photography/Superstock, Aflo
Co., Ltd./Alamy Stock Photo, Jose Luis Pelaez Inc/Getty Images, anouchka/
Getty Images; p.5 Pressmaster/Shutterstock, Vasily Pindyurin/Getty Images,
SuperStock, Max kegfire/Shutterstock; p.11 WAYHOME studio/Shutterstock,
Westend61/Superstock, Photographee.eu/Shutterstock, Blend Images/
Alamy Stock Photo, Tara Moore/Getty Images, nobelio/Shutterstock; p.13
Monkey Business Images/Shutterstock; p.19 Jonathan Larsen/Diadem
Images/Alamy Stock Photo, Hero Images/Superstock, Echo/Getty Images;
p.20 Ulrich Baumgarten/Contributor/Getty Images, Caia Images/Superstock,
Eugene Kocherva/Shutterstock, OJO Images Ltd/Alamy Stock Photo, Jose
Luis Pelaez Inc/Getty Images, Image Source/Getty Images, dolgachov/123rf,
Monkey Business Images/Shutterstock; p.27 Jonathan Larsen/Diadem
Images/Alamy Stock Photo; p.31 Hero Images/Getty Images; p.32 www.
rawsterne.co.uk, Anton_Ivanov/Shutterstock.com, Emilio Naranjo/EPA/
Newscom, Jeff Kravitz/Contributor/Getty Images, kecl/Getty Images, Kevin
M. McCarthy/Shutterstock.com, Jozef Sedmak/Shutterstock, ITAR-TASS
Photo Agency/Alamy Stock Photo; p.34 MATTES René/Hemis.fr/Superstock,
Hero Images/Superstock, Tyler Olson/Sjutterstock, Chad Ehlers/Alamy
Stock Photo, mediaphotos/Getty Images, MNStudio/Shutterstock, Meibion/
Alamy Stock Photo, S_L/Shutterstock; p.40 Anton Gvozdikov/Shutterstock.
com; p.43 Hero Images/Getty Images; p.44 science photo/Shutterstock,
Pressmaster/Shutterstock, Josh randall/Shutterstock, PHOVOIR/Alamy
Stock Photo, Monkey Business Images/Shutterstock, Zsolt Nyulaszi/Getty
Images, Rawpixel.com/Shutterstock, Panther Media GmbH/Alamy Stock
Photo; p.46, Moxie Productions/Getty Images, CREATISTA/Getty Images,
ASDF_MEDIA/Shutterstock, Neomaster/Shutterstock, Echo/Getty Images,
REUTERS/Alamy Stock Photo, Hero Images/Superstock, Panther Media
GmbH/Alamy Stock Photo; p.55 Hero Images/Getty Images; p.57 alexkich/
Shutterstock; mimagephotography/Shutterstock, photogal/Shutterstock;
p.58 SOMMAI/Shutterstock, alexkich/Shutterstock, leszekglasner/Getty
Images, Liljam/Shutterstock, Jiri Hera/Shutterstock, PhotoAlto/Superstock,
Tetra Images/Superstock, Feng Yu/Shutterstock; p.64 TorriPhoto/Getty
Images, Ray Kachatorian/Getty Images, rez-art/Getty Images, etorres/
Shutterstock, ji xiaoping/Shutterstock; p.67 wavebreakmedia/Shutterstock;
p.69 Hero Images/Getty Images; p.70 Jan Macuch/Shutterstock, Kvitka
Fabian/Shutterstock, Anastasiya Aleksandrenko/Shutterstock, asiseeit/
Getty Images, Maly Designer/Shutterstock, Funkystock/AGE footstock,
Ramon Espelt Gorgozo/Alamy Stock Photo, asiseeit/Getty Images; p.72
mimagephotography/Shutterstock, Andrey_Popov/Shutterstock, Gregory
James Van Raalte/Shutterstock, Adrian Sherratt/Alamy Stock Photo,
YAY Media AS/Alamy Stock Photo, ESB Professional/Shutterstock, Goran
Bogicevic/Shutterstock, Leonid S. Shtandel/Shutterstock; p.73 LauriPatterson/
Getty Images; p.81 Hero Images/Getty Images; p.82 ZUMA Press Inc/Alamy
Stock Photo, Zoom Team/Shutterstock, Dusan Kostic/Alamy Stock Photo,
Mode Images/Alamy Stock Photo, HONGQI ZHANG/123rf, JP Chretien/
Shutterstock, foodfolio/Alamy Stock Photo, photogal/Shutterstock; p.84
Steve Vidler/Superstock, dani3315/Shutterstock, Timothy G. Laman/
Contributor/Getty Images, Echo/Getty Images, HP Canada/Alamy Stock
Photo, andresr/Getty Images, Cultura Limited/Superstock, Photographee.eu/
Shutterstock; p.93 Hero Images/Getty Images; p.95 José Miguel Hernández
Hernández/Getty Images, NICOLAS HERRBACH/Alamy Stock Photo, MBI/
Alamy Stock Photo: p.96 Westend61 GmbH/Alamy Stock Photo, Peter
Gudella/Shutterstock, José Miguel Hernández Hernández/Getty Images,
Harri Tahvanainen/Folio Images/Getty Images, robertharding/Masterfile,
Photofusion/Contributor/Getty Images, Amelia Fox/Shutterstock, NorGal/
Shutterstock; p.98 age fotostock/Superstock, schulzie/Getty Images, Jeffrey
Blackler/Alamy Stock Photo, Jonathan Welch/Alamy Stock Photo, testing/
Shutterstock.com, Gabor Tinz/Shutterstock, Shih-Hao Liao/Alamy Stock
Photo, itakdalee/Shutterstock; p.107 Hero Images/Getty Images; p.108
NICOLAS HERRBACH/Alamy Stock Photo, wavebreakmedia/Shutterstock,
NetPhotos/Alamy Stock Photo, JuliusKielaitis/Shutterstock.com, STANCA
SANDA/Alamy Stock Photo, webpics/Alamy Stock Photo, Alex Segre/
Alamy Stock Photo, Visual Generation/Shutterstock; p.119 Hero Images/
Getty Images; p.120 GARO/PHANIE/Getty Images, Halfdark/Getty Images,
Ron Chapple Photography/Superstock, Jochen Tack/Alamy Stock Photo,
amphotora/Getty Images, Phanie/Alamy Stock Photo, MBI/Alamy Stock
Photo, Mega Pixel/Shutterstock; p.122 Seppo Hinkula/Alamy Stock Photo,
Serge Krouglikoff/Getty Images, gradyreese/Getty Images, Stokkete/
Shutterstock, Spencer Jones/Getty Images, Alice S./BSIP/Superstock,
Gregory_DUBUS/Getty Images, harper kt/Shutterstock; p.131 Hero Images/
Getty Images.

REVIEWERS

We would like to acknowledge the following individuals for their input during the development of the series:

Aubrey Adrianson
Ferris State University
U.S.A.

Sedat Akayoğlu
Middle East Technical
University
Turkey

Mahmoud Al-Salah
University of Dammam
Saudi Arabia

Lisa Alton
University of Alberta
Canada

Robert J. Ashcroft
Tokai University
Japan

Ibrahim Atay
Izzet Baysal University
Turkey

Türkan Aydin
Çanakkale Onsekiz Mart
University
Turkey

Pelin Tekinalp Cakmak
Marmara University, School of
Foreign Languages
Turkey

Raul Cantu
Austin Community College
United States

Karen E. Caldwell
Higher Colleges of Technology,
Women's College, U.A.E.

Danielle Chircop
Kaplan International English
U.S.A.

Jennifer Chung
Gwangju ECC
South Korea

Elaine Cockerham
Higher College of Technology
Oman

Abdullah Coskun
Abant Izzet Baysal University
Turkey

Stephanie da Costa Mello
Glendale Community College
U.S.A.

Travis Cote
Tamagawa University
Japan

Linda Crocker
University of Kentucky
U.S.A.

Ian Daniels
Smart ELT
Japan

Adem Onur Fedai
Fatih University Preparatory
School
Turkey

Gail Fernandez
Bergen Community College
U.S.A.

Theresa Garcia de Quevedo
Geos Boston English Language
School
U.S.A.

Greg Holloway
Kyushu Institute of Technology
Japan

Elizabeth Houtrow
Soongsil University
South Korea

Shu-Chen Huang
National Chengchi University
Taipei City

Patricia Ishill
Union County College
U.S.A.

Ji Hoon Kim
Independence English Institute
South Korea

Masakazu Kimura
Katoh Gakuen Gyoshu High
School/Nihon University
Japan

Georgios-Vlasios Kormpas
Al Yamamah University/SILC
Saudi Arabia

Ece Selva Küçükoğlu
METU School of Foreign
Languages
Turkey

Ji-seon Lee
Jeong English Campus
South Korea

Sang-lee Lee
Kangleong Community
Language Center
South Korea

Zee Eun Lim
Reader's Mate
South Korea

James MacDonald
Aspire Language Academy
Kaohsiung City

Margaret Martin
Xavier University
U.S.A.

Murray McMahon
University of Alberta
Canada

Chaker Ali Mhamdi
Al Buraimi University College
Oman

Elizabeth R. Neblett
Union County College
U.S.A.

Eileen O'Brien
Khalifa University of Science,
Technology and Research
U.A.E.

Fernanda Ortiz
Center for English as a Second
Language at University of
Arizona
U.S.A.

Ebru Osborne
Yildiz Technical University
Turkey

Joshua Pangborn
Kaplan International
U.S.A.

John Peloghitis
Tokai University
Japan

Erkan Kadir Şimşek
Akdeniz University Manavgat
Vocational College
Turkey

Veronica Struck
Sussex County Community
College
U.S.A.

Clair Taylor
Gifu Shotoku Gakuen
University
Japan

Melody Traylor
Higher Colleges of Technology
U.A.E.

Whitney Tullos
Intrax
U.S.A.

Sabiha Tunc
Baskent University English
Language Department
Turkey

John Vogels
Dubai Men's College
U.A.E.

Pingtang Yen
Eden Institute
Taichung City

Author Acknowledgments

The author wishes to express gratitude to the many people at Oxford University Press involved in the development of Trio Listening and Speaking 3. A very special thank you to John Evans and Sandra Frith who provided considerable editorial support throughout the writing process. The author would also like to thank Adam Wielopolski for providing much guidance at the final stages of this project.

—D.H.

CONTENTS

Welcome to Trio Listening and Speaking

Building Better Communicators . . . From the Beginning

Trio Listening and Speaking includes three levels of Student Books, Online Practice, and Teacher Support.

Level 1/CEFR A1

Level 2/CEFR A2

Level 3/CEFR B1

Essential Digital Content with Classroom Resources for Teachers

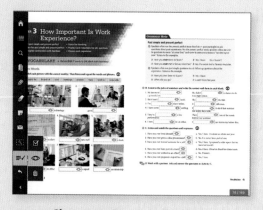

Classroom Presentation Tool

Trio Listening and Speaking's contextualized vocabulary instruction, academic listening strategies, and focus on pronunciation provide students with the tools they need for successful academic listening and speaking at the earliest stages of language acquisition.

Vocabulary Based On the Oxford 2000 ✐ Keywords

Trio Listening and Speaking's vocabulary is based on the 2,000 most important and useful words to learn at the early stages of language learning, making content approachable for low-level learners.

Practical Listening and Speaking Instruction

Conversation and academic listening sections prepare learners for real situations, while a focus on pronunciation helps students communicate successfully.

Readiness Unit

For added flexibility, each level of *Trio Listening and Speaking* begins with an optional Readiness Unit to provide fundamental English tools for beginning students.

INSIDE EACH CHAPTER

▲ VOCABULARY

Theme-based chapters set a context for learning.

Essential, explicit skills help beginning learners to gain confidence with listening and speaking.

Vocabulary is introduced in context and is built from the Oxford 2000 list of keywords.

The Grammar Note is matched closely to the listening and speaking tasks for supportive grammar instruction.

Trio Listening and Speaking Online Practice extends learning beyond the classroom, providing students with additional practice and support for each chapter's vocabulary, grammar, and skills instruction.

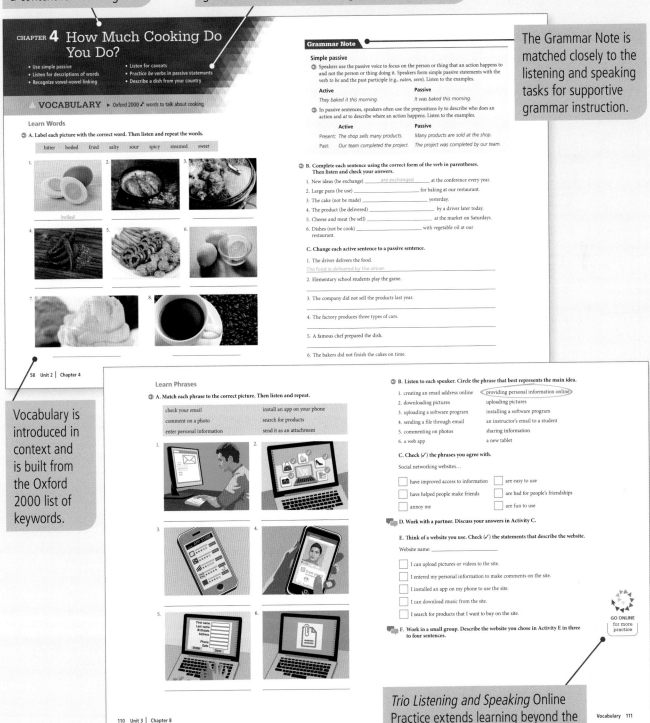

▲▲ LISTENING

Sounds of English boxes provide sound-symbol decoding practice and link fluency with listening and speaking skills to improve students' understanding of how English is really spoken.

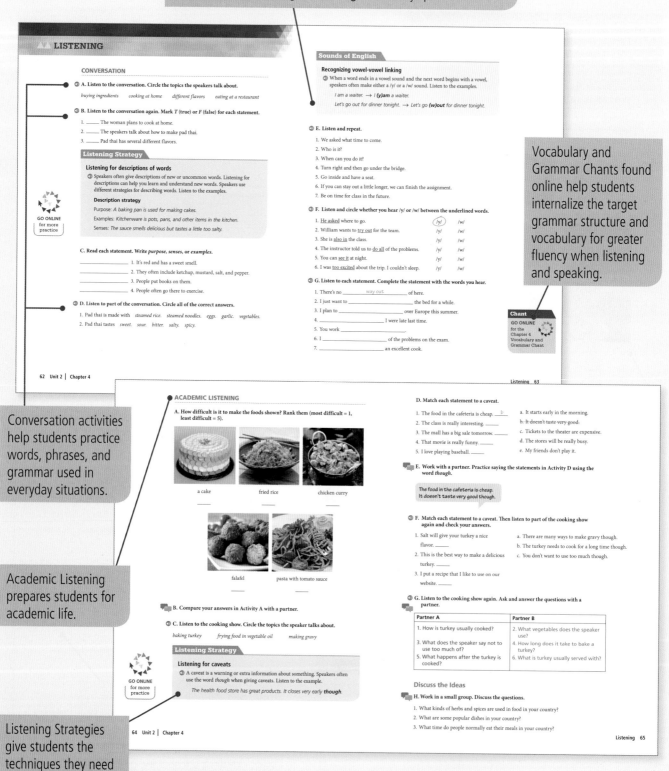

Vocabulary and Grammar Chants found online help students internalize the target grammar structure and vocabulary for greater fluency when listening and speaking.

Conversation activities help students practice words, phrases, and grammar used in everyday situations.

Academic Listening prepares students for academic life.

Listening Strategies give students the techniques they need to listen effectively.

▲▲ LISTENING

CONVERSATION

A. Listen to the conversation. Circle the topics the speakers talk about.

buying ingredients   cooking at home   different flavors   eating at a restaurant

B. Listen to the conversation again. Mark *T* (true) or *F* (false) for each statement.

1. _____ The woman plans to cook at home.
2. _____ The speakers talk about how to make pad thai.
3. _____ Pad thai has several different flavors.

Listening Strategy

Listening for descriptions of words

Speakers often give descriptions of new or uncommon words. Listening for descriptions can help you learn and understand new words. Speakers use different strategies for describing words. Listen to the examples.

Description strategy

Purpose: A baking pan is used for making cakes.
Examples: Kitchenware is pots, pans, and other items in the kitchen.
Senses: The sauce smells delicious but tastes a little too salty.

GO ONLINE for more practice

C. Read each statement. Write *purpose, senses,* or *examples.*

_____ 1. It's red and has a sweet smell.
_____ 2. They often include ketchup, mustard, salt, and pepper.
_____ 3. People put books on them.
_____ 4. People often go there to exercise.

D. Listen to part of the conversation. Circle all of the correct answers.

1. Pad thai is made with   steamed rice.   steamed noodles.   eggs.   garlic.   vegetables.
2. Pad thai tastes   sweet.   sour.   bitter.   salty.   spicy.

62   Unit 2 | Chapter 4

Sounds of English

Recognizing vowel-vowel linking

When a word ends in a vowel sound and the next word begins with a vowel, speakers often make either a /y/ or a /w/ sound. Listen to the examples.

I am a waiter. → I **(y)am** a waiter.
Let's go out for dinner tonight. → Let's go **(w)out** for dinner tonight.

E. Listen and repeat.

1. We asked what time to come.
2. Who is it?
3. When can you do it?
4. Turn right and then go under the bridge.
5. Go inside and have a seat.
6. If you can stay out a little longer, we can finish the assignment.
7. Be on time for class in the future.

F. Listen and circle whether you hear /y/ or /w/ between the underlined words.

1. He asked where to go.   (/y/)   /w/
2. William wants to try out for the team.   /y/   /w/
3. She is also in the class.   /y/   /w/
4. The instructor told us to do all of the problems.   /y/   /w/
5. You can see it at night.   /y/   /w/
6. I was too excited about the trip. I couldn't sleep.   /y/   /w/

G. Listen to each statement. Complete the statement with the words you hear.

1. There's no ___way out___ of here.
2. I just want to _____ the bed for a while.
3. I plan to _____ over Europe this summer.
4. _____ I were late last time.
5. You work _____
6. I _____ of the problems on the exam.
7. _____ an excellent cook.

Chant
GO ONLINE for the Chapter 4 Vocabulary and Grammar Chant

Listening   63

● ACADEMIC LISTENING

A. How difficult is it to make the foods shown? Rank them (most difficult = 1, least difficult = 5).

a cake   fried rice   chicken curry

falafel   pasta with tomato sauce

B. Compare your answers in Activity A with a partner.

C. Listen to the cooking show. Circle the topics the speaker talks about.

baking turkey   frying food in vegetable oil   making gravy

Listening Strategy

Listening for caveats

A caveat is a warning or extra information about something. Speakers often use the word *though* when giving caveats. Listen to the example.

The health food store has great products. It closes very early **though**.

GO ONLINE for more practice

64   Unit 2 | Chapter 4

D. Match each statement to a caveat.

1. The food in the cafeteria is cheap. __b__   a. It starts early in the morning.
2. The class is really interesting. _____   b. It doesn't taste very good.
3. The mall has a big sale tomorrow. _____   c. Tickets to the theater are expensive.
4. That movie is really funny. _____   d. The stores will be really busy.
5. I love playing baseball. _____   e. My friends don't play it.

E. Work with a partner. Practice saying the statements in Activity D using the word *though.*

The food in the cafeteria is cheap.
It doesn't taste very good though.

F. Match each statement to a caveat. Then listen to part of the cooking show again and check your answers.

1. Salt will give your turkey a nice flavor. _____   a. There are many ways to make gravy though.
2. This is the best way to make a delicious turkey. _____   b. The turkey needs to cook for a long time though.
3. I put a recipe that I like to use on our website. _____   c. You don't want to use too much though.

G. Listen to the cooking show again. Ask and answer the questions with a partner.

Partner A	Partner B
1. How is turkey usually cooked?	2. What vegetables does the speaker use?
3. What does the speaker say not to use too much of?	4. How long does it take to bake a turkey?
5. What happens after the turkey is cooked?	6. What is turkey usually served with?

Discuss the Ideas

H. Work in a small group. Discuss the questions.

1. What kinds of herbs and spices are used in food in your country?
2. What are some popular dishes in your country?
3. What time do people normally eat their meals in your country?

Listening   65

SPEAKING

The Pronunciation Skill helps students to speak clearly and intelligibly.

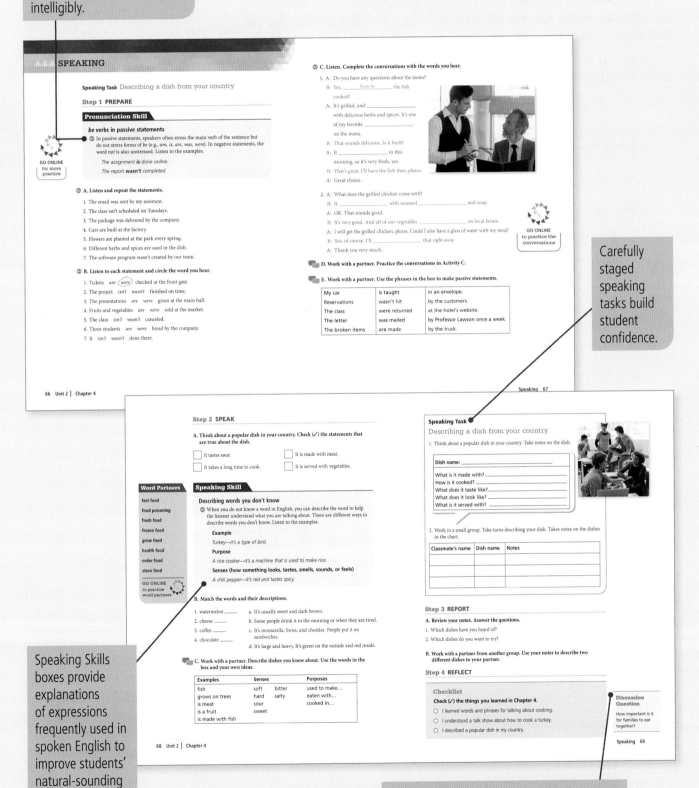

SPEAKING

Speaking Task Describing a dish from your country

Step 1 PREPARE

Pronunciation Skill

be verbs in passive statements

In passive statements, speakers often stress the main verb of the sentence but do not stress forms of *be* (e.g., *am, is, are, was, were*). In negative statements, the word *not* is also unstressed. Listen to the examples.

The assignment **is** done online.

The report **wasn't** completed.

GO ONLINE for more practice

A. Listen and repeat the statements.

1. The email was sent by my assistant.
2. The class isn't scheduled on Tuesdays.
3. The package was delivered by the company.
4. Cars are built at the factory.
5. Flowers are planted at the park every spring.
6. Different herbs and spices are used in the dish.
7. The software program wasn't created by our team.

B. Listen to each statement and circle the word you hear.

1. Tickets   *are* (*were*) checked at the front gate.
2. The project   *isn't   wasn't*   finished on time.
3. The presentations   *are   were*   given at the main hall.
4. Fruits and vegetables   *are   were*   sold at the market.
5. The class   *isn't   wasn't*   canceled.
6. Three students   *are   were*   hired by the company.
7. It   *isn't   wasn't*   done there.

66   Unit 2 | Chapter 4

C. Listen. Complete the conversations with the words you hear.

1. A: Do you have any questions about the menu?
   B: Yes, _____ *how is* _____ the fish cooked?
   A: It's grilled, and _____ with delicious herbs and spices. It's one of my favorite _____ on the menu.
   B: That sounds delicious. Is it fresh?
   A: It _____ in this morning, so it's very fresh, yes.
   B: That's great. I'll have the fish then, please.
   A: Great choice.

2. A: What does the grilled chicken come with?
   B: It _____ with steamed _____ and soup.
   A: OK. That sounds good.
   B: It's very good. And all of our vegetables _____ on local farms.
   A: I will get the grilled chicken, please. Could I also have a glass of water with my meal?
   B: Yes, of course. I'll _____ that right away.
   A: Thank you very much.

GO ONLINE to practice the conversations

D. Work with a partner. Practice the conversations in Activity C.

E. Work with a partner. Use the phrases in the box to make passive statements.

My car	is taught	in an envelope.
Reservations	wasn't hit	by the customers.
The class	were returned	at the hotel's website.
The letter	was mailed	by Professor Lawson once a week.
The broken items	are made	by the truck.

Speaking   67

Carefully staged speaking tasks build student confidence.

Step 2 SPEAK

A. Think about a popular dish in your country. Check (✓) the statements that are true about the dish.

☐ It tastes sour.
☐ It takes a long time to cook.
☐ It is made with meat.
☐ It is served with vegetables.

Word Partners

fast food
food poisoning
fresh food
frozen food
grow food
health food
order food
store food

GO ONLINE to practice word partners

Speaking Skill

Describing words you don't know

When you do not know a word in English, you can describe the word to help the listener understand what you are talking about. There are different ways to describe words you don't know. Listen to the examples.

Example
Turkey—it's a type of bird.

Purpose
A rice cooker—it's a machine that is used to make rice.

Senses (how something looks, tastes, smells, sounds, or feels)
A chili pepper—it's red and tastes spicy.

B. Match the words and their descriptions.

1. watermelon _____   a. It's usually sweet and dark brown.
2. cheese _____   b. Some people drink it in the morning or when they are tired.
3. coffee _____   c. It's mozzarella, Swiss, and cheddar. People put it on sandwiches.
4. chocolate _____   d. It's large and heavy. It's green on the outside and red inside.

C. Work with a partner. Describe dishes you know about. Use the words in the box and your own ideas.

Examples	Senses		Purposes
fish	soft	bitter	used to make...
grows on trees	hard	salty	eaten with...
is meat	sour		cooked in...
is a fruit	sweet		
is made with fish			

Speaking Skills boxes provide explanations of expressions frequently used in spoken English to improve students' natural-sounding speech.

68   Unit 2 | Chapter 4

Speaking Task

Describing a dish from your country

1. Think about a popular dish in your country. Take notes on the dish.

Dish name:
What is it made with?
How is it cooked?
What does it taste like?
What does it look like?
What is it served with?

2. Work in a small group. Take turns describing your dish. Takes notes on the dishes in the chart.

Classmate's name	Dish name	Notes

Step 3 REPORT

A. Review your notes. Answer the questions.

1. Which dishes have you heard of?
2. Which dishes do you want to try?

B. Work with a partner from another group. Use your notes to describe two different dishes to your partner.

Step 4 REFLECT

Checklist

Check (✓) the things you learned in Chapter 4.

○ I learned words and phrases for talking about cooking.
○ I understood a talk show about how to cook a turkey.
○ I described a popular dish in my country.

Discussion Question

How important is it for families to eat together?

Speaking   69

Students discuss a question in small groups to develop critical thinking skills.

ix

Trio Listening and Speaking Online Practice: Essential Digital Content

Trio Listening and Speaking Online Practice provides multiple opportunities for skills practice and acquisition—beyond the classroom and beyond the page.

Each unit of *Trio Listening and Speaking* is accompanied by a variety of automatically graded activities. Students' progress is recorded, tracked, and fed back to the instructor.

Vocabulary and Grammar Chants help students internalize the target grammar structure and vocabulary for greater accuracy and fluency when listening and speaking.

Vocabulary Oxford 2000 words to talk about cooking
Put the words in the correct order to make a sentence.

1. made | this | pepper | dish | is | chilli | with | .

2. salad | the | is | . | with | served | food

3. . | fresh | are | served | the | vegetables

4. the | with | lemon | . | he | dish | likes

5. the | some | salty | dish | is | for | too | people | .

6. . | in | cook | pan | meat | a | the | large

7. is | an | the | in | baked | oven | . | fish

8. bitter | has | . | dish | the | a | taste

Try again   Reset   Submit

> Online Activities provide essential practice of Vocabulary, Grammar, Listening, Speaking, and Pronunication.

> GO ONLINE icons lead students to essential digital content.

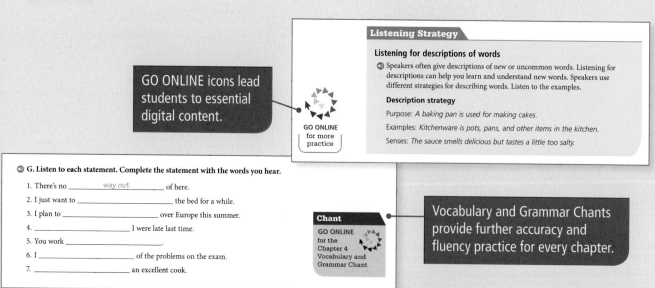

GO ONLINE for more practice

Listening Strategy

Listening for descriptions of words

Speakers often give descriptions of new or uncommon words. Listening for descriptions can help you learn and understand new words. Speakers use different strategies for describing words. Listen to the examples.

Description strategy

Purpose: *A baking pan is used for making cakes.*

Examples: *Kitchenware is pots, pans, and other items in the kitchen.*

Senses: *The sauce smells delicious but tastes a little too salty.*

G. Listen to each statement. Complete the statement with the words you hear.

1. There's no _____way out_____ of here.
2. I just want to _____ the bed for a while.
3. I plan to _____ over Europe this summer.
4. _____ I were late last time.
5. You work _____ .
6. I _____ of the problems on the exam.
7. _____ an excellent cook.

Chant
GO ONLINE for the Chapter 4 Vocabulary and Grammar Chant

> Vocabulary and Grammar Chants provide further accuracy and fluency practice for every chapter.

Use the access code on the inside front cover to log in at **www.oxfordlearn.com/login**.

Readiness Unit

Vocabulary

Nouns, verbs, and adjectives
Activities
Present progressive
Simple past tense
Present perfect
Adjectives and prepositions

Listening

Contractions
Weak forms
Tone and attitude
Listening for main ideas
Sequence phrases

Speaking

Syllable stress
Intonation in questions
Turn-taking phrases
Requests with *could*
Discussing plans

UNIT WRAP UP Extend Your Skills

Nouns, verbs, and adjectives

A. Complete the chart.

Noun	Verb	Adjective
challenge	challenge	challenging
danger		_____
_____	exercise	
_____		healthy
ownership	_____	
_____	pollute	polluted
preparation	_____	prepared
safety		safe
savings	_____	
value	value	_____
work	_____	working

B. Circle the correct form of the word.

1. The video game was   challenge.   (challenging.)

2. Some sports can be   danger.   dangerous.

3. The snack is not very   health.   healthy.

4. The river is   pollution.   polluted.

◑ C. Complete each sentence with a word from the chart in Activity A. Then listen and check your answers.

1.

I _____ _work_ _____
at a bank.

2.

The app _____
me a lot of time.

3.

I _____
a small apartment.

4.

I stay _____ by eating fruits and vegetables.

5.

The exam was very _____.

6.

Cyclists wear helmets to stay _____.

Activities

A. Match the verbs and nouns. Then listen and check your answers.

1. go   in a gym
2. do   a bicycle
3. play   hiking
4. exercise   swimming
5. ride   yoga
6. go   tennis

B. Match each phrase in Activity A with the correct picture.

C. Complete each sentence with an activity from the box.

basketball	bowling	golfing	hockey	~~martial arts~~

1. I do _____ martial arts _____ on the weekends at the gym.

2. I like to go _____ at a place in the mall.

3. You can play _____ at the outdoor ice rink.

4. We plan to play _____ on one of the courts at the athletic center.

5. We went _____ this morning, but the weather was rainy, and the course was very wet.

D. Work with a partner. Which activities do you like to do? Take turns asking and answering questions.

> Which activities do you like to do?

> I like to play golf. I play about once a month. What activities do you do?

> I play basketball. My roommate and I play all the time.

Present progressive

Speakers use the form *am/is/are* + *-ing* verb to describe actions happening now and to describe future plans.

A. Complete each sentence with the correct form of the present progressive of the verb in parentheses. Then listen and check your answers.

1.

I (work) _____ am working _____ tonight.

2.

He (eat) _____ right now.

3.

(go) _____ you

_____ to class

this afternoon?

4.

Elaine (not study)

_____ finance at

college.

5.

(read) _____ she

_____ in the

library?

6.

The computer (not work)

_____ today.

B. Listen and match the questions and responses.

1. What are you doing tonight?   I'm meeting Tian.

2. Who are you meeting?   I'm going shopping.

3. Where are you going shopping?   My favorite store is having a sale.

4. Why are you going there?   I'm going to Somerset Mall.

C. Work with a partner. Take turns asking and answering the questions in Activity B.

Simple past tense

Past time markers tell you when an action was completed in the past. Past time markers often go with the simple past tense.

A. Listen and match the statements and past time markers.

1. I visited the art museum   yesterday.

2. She did not go to Europe   last week.

3. They finished the project   three years ago.

4. They played sports together   when they were children.

5. He came to the United States   in September.

6. Our team met   last year.

B. Complete each sentence with the correct form of the verb in parentheses.

1. I (go) _____ went _____ abroad for the first time two years ago.

2. She (not answer) _____ the question on the exam yesterday.

3. I (wake up) _____ very early this morning.

4. We (have) _____ time to go to the museum last summer.

5. They (go) _____ on a hike last week.

6. (go) _____ you _____ to class yesterday?

C. Match the past tense verbs and phrases.

1. had   a close game
2. won   a good time
3. solved   a risk
4. took   a museum
5. visited   a difficult problem

D. Write simple past statements about things you did. Then share your statements with a partner.

1. _____ yesterday.

2. _____ last weekend.

3. _____ a week ago.

4. _____ last summer.

E. Work with a partner. Use the words in the chart to ask and answer simple past questions.

Question words	Verbs		Time markers
what	go	wake up	last weekend
when	do	eat	yesterday
where	meet		this morning
who			last night

What did you do last weekend?

I played hockey with some friends.

Present perfect

The present perfect tense uses the form *have/has* + past participle verb. Past participle verbs often end in *-ed*, but there are other irregular past participle verbs that have different endings.

A. Complete the chart with the irregular past participle forms.

Simple form	Past simple	Past participle
go	went	*gone*
meet	met	_____
have	had	_____
see	saw	_____
take	took	_____
eat	ate	_____
be	was/were	_____
do	did	_____

B. Listen and complete each statement with the past participle verb you hear.

1. She has _____ *been* _____ to Canada.

2. They have _____ the movie.

3. Paul has _____ at the new restaurant.

4. We have _____ the train to Chicago.

5. I haven't _____ the new instructor.

6. Have you ever _____ yoga?

7. She hasn't _____ swimming this week.

8. We haven't _____ a vacation yet.

C. Put each set of words in the correct order to form a statement or question. Then listen and check your answers.

1. she / the assignment / has / done / ?

   Has she done the assignment?

2. eaten / not / have / it / I

   _____

3. they / have / met / ?

_____

4. been to / Mexico / we / have

_____

5. have / taken / the train / we / three times this week

_____

6. has not / the movie / seen / she

_____

Adjectives and prepositions

Speakers often use the form *be* + adjective + preposition to describe things.

A. Listen to each statement and circle the preposition you hear.

1. Sean is interested (in) about apps.
2. They're excited to about their trip.
3. I was surprised in by my grade.
4. The city is famous for with its museums.
5. They were nervous about with the exam.
6. Mike was worried in about the weather.

B. Complete each question with the correct preposition.

1. Are you excited _____ *about* _____ this class?
2. Are you nervous _____ taking this class?
3. Are you responsible _____ homework in this class?
4. Are you interested _____ studying foreign languages?
5. Are you worried _____ tests in this class?

C. Ask and answer the questions in Activity B with a partner.

Are you excited about this class?

Yes, I am.

Contractions

Speakers often use contractions in conversation. Contractions usually combine a pronoun and a helping verb into a shorter form.

he will go	*he'll go*
they have done	*they've done*
it is	*it's*

A. Listen and repeat the contracted form of each statement.

1. He is leaving now.

2. She would like to come.

3. They have been there.

4. They will not join us.

5. She is going to the game.

6. She has not seen the movie.

7. I cannot find the book.

8. We are going to go to the museum.

B. Listen to the statements in Activity A again. Underline the words that are contracted in each sentence.

C. Write the contraction for the underlined words in each statement. Then listen and check your answers.

1. <u>It will</u> rain tomorrow. _____It'll_____

2. <u>She would</u> like to come. _____

3. <u>They have</u> been there. _____

4. They <u>did not</u> finish. _____

5. She <u>was not</u> at the event. _____

6. <u>They are</u> going to visit. _____

7. <u>We have</u> done the assignment. _____

8. <u>I am</u> not going to go to the game. _____

 **D. Listen to the short conversations. Then practice them with a partner.**

1. A: Did you finish the assignment?

   B: No, I didn't have time.

   A: I haven't done it either. I'm planning to do it tonight.

   B: I don't have time tonight. I'll probably finish it over the weekend.

2. A: Do you want to practice the dialogue with me?

   B: I'm sorry. I don't understand. What does *dialogue* mean?

   A: It's a conversation or discussion between two or more people.

   B: Oh, OK. I'll go first then!

Weak forms

Weak forms are words that are unstressed. Weak forms are often small words and are less important. Strong forms are words that are stressed and carry meaning in a sentence.

The students would like to try it.   The students would like-ta try it.

Examples of weak forms
to, for, at, in
a, an, the
can, could, do, does, am, be, have, has, was, were

A. Listen and repeat.

1. Could you give me a minute to think?

2. They like to do extreme sports.

3. I had to work last night.

4. He was not at the meeting in the morning.

5. The answer to the question is on page 5.

6. The exam is for all students in the class.

B. Underline the weak forms. Then listen and check your answers.

1. They <u>have</u> worked <u>on the</u> project <u>for an</u> hour.

2. I have to go to the bank.

3. We did not find an apartment.

4. You can find it at the store.

5. He is looking for his shoes.

6. It is an interesting idea.

 C. Work with a partner. Practice saying the sentences in Activity B.

Tone and attitude

Speakers often express their feelings through how they say a word or phrase.

A. Match the words in the box with the pictures.

| anger | disgust | dislike | excitement | sadness | surprise |

1. _____
   excitement

2. _____

3. _____

4. _____

5. _____

6. _____

B. Listen to each statement. Write the word from the box that describes the speaker's attitude.

| anger | disgust | dislike | excitement | sadness | surprise |

____surprise____ 1. So, you're coming?

_____ 2. He's here now.

_____ 3. I lost my favorite jacket.

_____ 4. I don't enjoy playing golf at all.

_____ 5. That food is two days old.

_____ 6. The train was late again.

C. Listen to each statement. Circle the word that describes the speaker's attitude.

1. The package finally arrived?   surprise   disgust

2. I got a B on the test.   excitement   anger

3. Has the food been sitting outside all this time?   sadness   disgust

4. That dish is $20.   dislike   excitement

5. She's planning to come to the game tomorrow.   surprise   dislike

Listening for main ideas

🔊 **A. Listen to part of the talk. Check (✓) the main idea.**

☐ The speaker talks about bowling.

☐ The speaker talks about weekend hobbies.

☐ The speaker likes to play sports.

🔊 **B. Think about the talk in Activity A. Predict what the speaker will talk about next. Then listen and check your answer.**

☐ how to join a team

☐ the benefits of sports

☐ people's hobbies and free time

Sequence phrases

Speakers often use sequence phrases to explain the order of events.

A. Put the words and phrases in the box in the correct columns in the chart.

at first	at the start	finally	in the end
next	second	then	to begin	to finish

First	Next	Last

🔊 **B. Listen to the short conversation. Number the statements in the correct order.**

_____ I went grocery shopping.

_____ I went to the bank.

_____ I had a chance to relax at home.

_____ I worked out the gym.

Syllable stress

Speakers stress syllables in words. Using the correct stress helps listeners understand what speakers are saying.

A. Write how many syllables are in each word.

1. partner ___2___

2. instructor _____

3. textbook _____

4. classroom _____

5. discussion _____

6. assignment _____

7. presentation _____

8. pencil _____

B. Listen and circle the stressed syllable.

1. partner

2. instructor

3. textbook

4. classroom

5. discussion

6. assignment

7. presentation

8. pencil

C. Complete each statement. Then listen and check your answers.

1. Work with a ___partner___.

2. Give a _____.

3. Close your _____.

4. Ask the _____ a question.

5. Complete an _____.

6. Have a _____.

7. Look around the _____.

8. Find a _____.

 D. Work with a partner. Practice the statements in Activity C.

Speaking 13

Intonation in questions

When speakers ask *yes/no* questions, their intonation rises. However, when speakers ask *wh-* questions, their intonation falls. Listen to the examples.

Are you from Denmark?   Where are you from?

A. Listen to each question. Does the intonation rise or fall? Draw (↗) for rising intonation and (↘) for falling intonation.

1. Where are you from?

2. Is it nice there?

3. What are you studying?

4. Do you like it?

5. Where do you live?

6. Is it a good place?

7. What do you do for fun?

8. Is it difficult to do?

B. Listen. Complete each short conversation with the words you hear.

1. A: Where do you _____live_____?

   B: I live in a dormitory on campus.

   A: Is it _____?

   B: It's not bad.

2. A: What are you _____?

   B: I'm studying statistics.

   A: Do you like the _____?

   B: The courses are good, but they are difficult.

3. A: What do you do for _____?

   B: I usually play tennis.

   A: Oh, do you play at the student fitness _____?

   B: No, I usually go to the park.

C. Practice the short conversations in Activity B with a partner. Make the responses to the questions true for you.

Where do you live?

I live in an apartment off campus.

Is it nice?

Yes, I like it, but the rent is high.

Turn-taking phrases

Students often work with a partner or group in class. When working with others, students use turn-taking phrases to include everyone in a conversation. Listen to the examples.

Do you want to start?   *I think it's your turn.*

A. Match the questions and responses. Then listen and check your answers.

1. Is it OK if I go first?   I can do the first part.

2. What do you think?   OK, thanks.

3. Who's next?   I'll go next.

4. Which one do you want to do?   Sure. Not a problem.

5. I think it's your turn.   I think it's a good idea.

B. Listen. Complete the short conversations with the words you hear.

1. A: Do you have a _____partner_____?
   B: No, I don't.
   A: Do you want to practice this dialogue _____?
   B: Sure. That _____ good.
   A: Do you _____ to take part B?
   B: That's _____ with me.

2. A: Do you want to go _____?
   B: Sure. I'll _____, but my answer is kind of short.
   A: That's OK. _____ is mine.

3. A: What did you _____ for question 1?
   B: I chose _____ B.
   A: Oh, so _____ I.
   B: Do you want to _____ to the next question?
   A: Yeah, we're running out _____ time.

4. A: Do you want to _____ question 1?
   B: Yes, that's no _____. Are you going to do question 2 then?
   A: Sure. I'll _____ question 2.
   B: Great.

C. Work with a partner. Practice the conversations in Activity B.

Requests with *could*

A polite way to make a request is to use the word *could*. Listen to the example.

Could you explain the assignment again?

A. Listen and complete the questions with the words from the box.

check	explain	help	play	say	spell

1. Could you _____ help _____ me with this question?
2. Could you _____ that again?
3. Could you _____ that one more time?
4. Could you _____ the recording again?
5. Could you _____ my answers?
6. Could you _____ that word?

B. Listen and circle the responses you hear.

1. Could you help me with this question?
   a. Sure. How can I help you?   b. Sure. What are you having trouble with?

2. Could you say that again?
   a. Yes, the assignment is due next week.   b. Of course. The assignment is due next Monday.

3. Could you play the recording again?
   a. I will play it again at the end of the exercise.   b. Yes, just one second.

4. Could you check my answers?
   a. Yes, I can do it after class.   b. Yes, I'll look at them during the break.

C. Complete the conversation with the words from the box. Then practice the conversation with a partner.

help	problem	spell	trouble

A: Excuse me. Could you _____ me with this question?

B: Of course. What are you having _____ with?

A: Could you _____ *assignment*?

B: It's spelled A - S - S - I - G - N - M - E - N - T.

A: Thank you very much.

B: No _____ .

Discussing plans

When speakers talk about future plans, they often use the phrase *be going to* + verb. The word *to* is unstressed in the statements. For negative statements with *be going to* + verb, the negative (*not/isn't/aren't*) is stressed. Listen to the examples.

I'm going to meet a friend later today.   *She isn't going to attend the event.*

A. Listen and circle the answers you hear. Then listen again and repeat the statements.

1. A: What are you going to do tonight?
   B: I'm going to the   *mall.*   *park.*

2. A: What are his plans for this summer?
   B: He's going to   *travel abroad.*   *stay at home.*

3 A: Where are they going to live?
   B: They're going to live in   *an apartment.*   *a house.*

4. A: Are you taking the class next semester?
   B: No, I'm not taking the class until   *next year.*   *next spring.*

5. A: Where is she buying the food for the party?
   B: She's buying it   *at the grocery store.*   *at a market.*

6. A: Are they going to the beach this weekend?
   B: No, they're not going to the beach. They're going to the   *theater.*   *game.*

B. Match the questions and answers.

1. Where are you going to go this weekend?   I am going to come back on Sunday night.

2. Who are you going to go with?   I am going to take a bus.

3. What time are you going to leave?   I am going to go with some friends.

4. How are you going to get there?   I am going to leave early in the morning.

5. When are you going to come back?   I am going to go camping in the mountains.

C. Work with a partner. Take turns asking and answering the questions in Activity B.

D. Circle the answer that is true for you. Then ask and answer the questions with a partner.

1. Are you going to study after class?   *Yes, I am.*   *No, I'm not.*

2. Are you going to watch a movie after class?   *Yes, I am.*   *No, I'm not.*

3. Are you going to have dinner after class?   *Yes, I am.*   *No, I'm not.*

4. Are you going to meet a friend after class?   *Yes, I am.*   *No, I'm not.*

5. Are you going to work out after class?   *Yes, I am.*   *No, I'm not.*

Look at the word bank for the Readiness Unit. Check (✓) the words you know. Circle the words you want to learn better.

OXFORD 2000 🔑

Adjectives	Nouns	Verbs	
close	apartment	answer	swim
correct	bicycle	close	take
dangerous	danger	discuss	win
difficult	discussion	do	
excited	exam	go	
famous	idea	have	
good	library	make	
important	museum	plan	
interesting	problem	play	
nervous	team	prepare	
responsible	theater	ride	
surprised	turn	save	
worried		solve	

PRACTICE WITH THE OXFORD 2000 🔑

A. Use the chart. Match adjectives with nouns.

1. _an important discussion_   2. _____

3. _____   4. _____

5. _____   6. _____

B. Use the chart. Match verbs with nouns.

1. _go to the library_   2. _____

3. _____   4. _____

5. _____   6. _____

C. Use the chart. Match verbs with adjective noun partners.

1. _solve difficult problems_   2. _____

3. _____   4. _____

5. _____   6. _____

UNIT **1** Personal and Professional Experience

CHAPTER **1** ## Do You Enjoy Challenges?

△ **VOCABULARY**
- Oxford 2000 🔑 words to talk about challenges and experiences

△△ **LISTENING**
- Listening for a speaker's mood
- Listening for phrases that signal emphasis

△△△ **SPEAKING**
- Practicing -ed sounds for past tense verbs
- Discussing challenges in college

CHAPTER **2** ## Can Art Improve a Person's Life?

△ **VOCABULARY**
- Oxford 2000 🔑 words to talk about art and leisure

△△ **LISTENING**
- Listening for follow-up comments
- Listening for phrases that signal order

△△△ **SPEAKING**
- Practicing syllable stress
- Making suggestions for an arts and culture project on campus

CHAPTER **3** ## How Important Is Work Experience?

△ **VOCABULARY**
- Oxford 2000 🔑 words to talk about work experience

△△ **LISTENING**
- Listening for past simple and present perfect
- Listening for chunking

△△△ **SPEAKING**
- Practicing verb reductions for *wh-* questions
- Discussing work experience

UNIT WRAP UP ## Extend Your Skills

CHAPTER 1 Do You Enjoy Challenges?

- Use verbs with *-ing* and *to*
- Listen for a speaker's mood
- Recognize reduction of weak forms
- Listen for phrases that signal emphasis
- Practice *-ed* sounds for past tense verbs
- Discuss challenges in college

▲ VOCABULARY ► Oxford 2000 🔑 words to talk about challenges and experiences

Learn Words

🔊 **A. Label each picture with the correct word(s). Then listen and repeat the words and phrases.**

| a business   a competition   an exam   ~~a foreign language~~   home   married   a new job   a presentation |

1.

learn ___a foreign language___

2.

enter _____

3.

get _____

4.

have _____

5.

start _____

6.

get _____

7.

give _____

8.

move into a new _____

Grammar Note

Verbs with -ing and to

After some verbs, speakers use verb + -ing. Speakers also use infinitive + to after some types of verbs. Listen to the examples.

Verb + gerund

enjoy + verb(-ing)	→	Leia doesn't enjoy playing basketball.
finish + verb(-ing)	→	He finished studying.

Verb + infinitive

need + to verb	→	I need to buy some new running shoes.
decide + to verb	→	She decided to help me.

B. Listen to each statement. Write the correct verb form.

1. I need _____ *to go* _____ home at six.

2. She hopes _____ married next year.

3. Farook plans on _____ engineering.

4. I wanted _____ a business, but it was too difficult.

5. When I was in college, I hated _____ for tests.

C. Listen and match the questions and answers.

1. What do you like to do on the weekend? __*d*__   a. I plan to study abroad in Australia.

2. What are you going to do this summer? _____   b. I need to prepare for a test.

3. What are you doing later tonight? _____   c. I would like to learn a foreign language.

4. What are you doing over the break? _____   d. I enjoy playing sports.

D. Work with a partner. Ask and answer the questions in Activity C.

E. Write the correct form of the verb in parentheses. Then listen and check your answers.

1. A: What did you enjoy (do) _____ *doing* _____ while you were there?

   B: I enjoyed (learn) _____ the language.

2. A: Where would she like (go) _____ this weekend?

   B: She would like (visit) _____ the art gallery.

3. What do you hope (do) _____ after college?

   B: I plan (start) _____ my own business.

4. A: Why do you avoid (take) _____ risks?

   B: I need (be) _____ careful.

Learn Phrases

A. Match each phrase to the correct picture. Then listen and repeat.

avoid trying new foods	learn to play an instrument
climb to the top of a mountain	live on your own
dislike danger	run a race
face a challenge	take surfing lessons

1.

2.

3.

"No way!"

4.

5.

6.

7.

8.

B. Listen to the speakers. Circle the phrase that completes each sentence.

1. The speaker   *moved abroad.*   *(didn't move abroad.)*

2. The speaker   *likes to take risks.*   *avoids risks.*

3. Midori   *took surfing lessons.*   *did not take surfing lessons.*

4. The speaker believes   *new challenges are hard at first.*   *new challenges are always hard.*

5. Ji-soo's new business   *is doing well.*   *is not doing well.*

6. The father   *likes trying new foods.*   *does not like trying new foods.*

7. The speaker   *entered a competition.*   *won a competition.*

C. Check (✓) the phrase that best matches you or your opinion. Then share your answers with a partner.

1. ☐ I avoid taking risks.   ☐ I am not afraid to take risks.

2. ☐ Climbing to the top of a mountain is interesting.   ☐ Climbing to the top of a mountain is boring.

3. ☐ I like trying new foods.   ☐ I don't like trying new foods.

4. ☐ Starting a new business is a bad idea.   ☐ Starting a new business is a good idea.

5. ☐ I enjoy new experiences.   ☐ I don't like new experiences.

6. ☐ Skydiving is dangerous.   ☐ Skydiving is not dangerous.

7. ☐ Learning a foreign language is boring.   ☐ Learning a foreign language is interesting.

8. ☐ It's important to get married.   ☐ It's not important to get married.

D. Work in a small group. Discuss the questions.

1. What challenges do international students face when they move abroad?

2. What was your best experience in high school?

3. What sport would you like to take lessons in?

GO ONLINE
for more
practice

▲▲ LISTENING

CONVERSATION

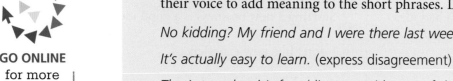 **A. Listen to the conversation. Circle the items that the speakers talk about.**

the weekend   *skydiving*   *the summer weather*   *surfing*

🔊 **B. Listen to the conversation again. Circle the correct answers.**

1. What did John do?   *went skydiving*   *entered a competition*

2. Why didn't Mukesh go   *The weather was bad.*   *Mukesh dislikes*
   skydiving?   *adventure sports.*

3. What did Mukesh do over   *went skydiving*   *took surfing lessons*
   the weekend?

Listening Strategy

Listening for a speaker's mood

🔊 Speakers often use short phrases to describe how they feel. They also change
their voice to add meaning to the short phrases. Listen to the examples.

No kidding? My friend and I were there last weekend. (express surprise)

It's actually easy to learn. (express disagreement)

That's true, but it's fun. (disagree with part of the statement)

GO ONLINE
for more
practice

🔊 **C. Listen to part of the conversation again. Circle the word that best describes
each speaker's mood.**

1. Really? My friend and I planned to go skydiving last Friday.

surprise   *agreement*   *disagreement*   *fear*

2. Well, if the weather is bad, it might be a little dangerous.

surprise   *agreement*   *disagreement*   *interest*

3. Good to know. I'm going to have to do it someday.

surprise   *agreement*   *interest*   *emphasis*

D. Listen to part of the conversation again. For each sentence, choose a word from the box that describes the speaker's mood. You will not use all of the words.

| agreement | disagreement | emphasis | fear | interest | surprise |

1. OK, listen to this. _____

2. Oh wow, that sounds fun. _____

3. Yeah, I have an exam today. _____

Sounds of English

Reduction of weak forms

Weak forms are short words that speakers say quickly, such as *to, for,* and *an*. Weak forms usually do not carry meaning in a sentence. Listen to the examples.

He decided to go. → He decided **ta** go.

I'm going for a bike ride. → I'm going **fora** bike ride.

The trip takes about an hour. → The trip takes about **en** hour.

E. Listen and repeat.

1. The boys wanted to try the new restaurant.

2. Could I have an orange juice?

3. They are going on an adventure.

4. He has lived here for a long time.

5. I had to study for an exam.

6. He went for a coffee at 11 AM.

F. Listen to each question or statement. Write the weak form you hear.

1. Are you going _____*to*_____ the gym tonight?

2. Do _____ like facing challenges?

3. I don't know what _____ do.

4. He has been living abroad _____ a long time.

5. Would you like _____ apple?

G. Work with a partner. Ask and answer the questions.

1. What did you like to do when you were in high school?

2. How many hours a week did you plan to study for this class?

3. When did you begin studying English?

What did you like to do when you were in high school?   I liked to play soccer.

Chant

GO ONLINE
for the
Chapter 1
Vocabulary and
Grammar Chant

ACADEMIC LISTENING

 A. Read each item. Rank the following actions (very challenging = 6, not challenging = 1). Then compare your answers with a partner.

_____ starting a business with your own money _____ learning a foreign language

_____ trying a food that you have never seen before _____ going skydiving

_____ going surfing _____ moving abroad

 B. Work in a small group. Ask and answer questions about the items in Activity A.

1. Do you like trying new foods?

2. What country do you want to visit most?

3. What is hard about moving abroad?

4. Which adventure sports do you like?

C. Listen to the first part of the lecture. Circle the correct answers.

1. The professor says that challenges can help us   *enjoy life.*   *learn new things.*

2. The professor says people have   *similar*   *different*   feelings about challenges.

3. People who love risk usually   *are better at learning new things*   *like adventure sports.*

D. Listen to the whole lecture. Take notes in the chart.

People who like challenges and danger	People who don't like challenges and danger
1. start new businesses	1. avoid _____ risks
2. _____ abroad	2. avoid _____ a new business
3. like _____ sports	3. dislike _____
4. learn _____	

> ### Listening Strategy
>
> ## Listening for phrases that signal emphasis
>
> Speakers often use short phrases to emphasize important points or information. Listen to the examples.
>
> **One thing to know** *is that you must apply early.*
>
> **The point** *is that the book is free.*

GO ONLINE
for more
practice

E. Listen to part of the lecture again. Complete each sentence with a phrase from the box.

But it is important to remember   Now don't forget   Now I'd like to point out that

1. _____ this can also have bad results.

2. _____ this can also mean people miss fun new experiences.

3. _____ the assignment is due at the beginning of next class.

F. Work with a partner. Ask and answer the questions.

Partner A	Partner B
1. What is the main topic of the lecture?	2. What two types of people does the professor discuss?
3. Why do some people like new challenges?	4. Why do some people dislike challenges?
5. What kind of assignment does the professor give?	6. When is the assignment due?

What is the main topic of the lecture?

The lecture is about taking risks and facing challenges.

Discuss the Ideas

G. Work in a small group. Which sports are challenging in your opinion? Complete the first column in the chart.

Challenging sports	Why are they challenging?
1. _____	
2. _____	
3. _____	

H. Work in a small group. Complete the second column in the chart in Activity G.

Listening   27

▲▲▲ SPEAKING

Speaking Task Discussing challenges in college

Step 1 PREPARE

Pronunciation Skill

-ed sounds for past tense verbs

◑ Speakers pronounce the *-ed* ending of a regular past tense verb in three different ways: /t/, /d/, and /id/. Listen to the examples.

/t/
I **worked** last night.

/d/
She **exercised** at the gym.

/id/
They **waited** for instructions.

GO ONLINE
for more
practice

◑ **A. Listen and complete each sentence.**

1. We _____worked_____ on the project all night.

2. He _____ to play basketball.

3. She _____ working there.

4. Phil _____ tired.

5. Serena _____ to start her own business.

6. I _____ to go skydiving, but the weather was bad.

7. The student _____ for the book.

◑ **B. Listen to the sentences in Activity A and repeat.**

◑ **C. Listen to each word. Circle the type of -ed sound you hear.**

1. needed	/t/	(/id/)	/d/	2. enjoyed	/t/ /id/ /d/
3. walked	/t/	/id/	/d/	4. avoided	/t/ /id/ /d/
5. cooked	/t/	/id/	/d/	6. hated	/t/ /id/ /d/
7. loved	/t/	/id/	/d/	8. visited	/t/ /id/ /d/
9. wanted	/t/	/id/	/d/	10. waited	/t/ /id/ /d/

🔊 **D. Predict the -ed sound for each underlined word. Then listen and check your answers.**

| /t/ | /id/ | /d/ |

1. She <u>planted</u> a tree in the yard. _/id/_ 2. She <u>played</u> soccer. _____

3. The boy <u>pushed</u> his friend. _____ 4. The doctor <u>treated</u> him. _____

5. We already <u>booked</u> a room. _____ 6. They <u>listened</u> to music last night. _____

🔊 **E. Listen. Complete each conversation with the words from the box.**

1. | ~~loved~~   needed   studied   visited   wanted |

A: How was your trip last weekend?

B: I _____ loved _____ it. It was a lot of fun, and I _____

a break from my studies.

A: Where did you go?

B: We _____ Pentwater. It's a small town.

A: Why did you go there?

B: Well, we _____ to go there because the town has a beautiful

beach and very nice restaurants. So, what did you do last weekend?

A: Well, I _____ at home all weekend.

B: Sorry to hear that.

A: Me too.

2. | arrived   called   happened   needed   planned   waited |

A: So, where were you this afternoon?

B: I went to the mall. I _____ to buy a winter coat.

A: Good idea. It's already getting cold. Did you go with Raul?

B: No, we _____ to meet at the bus stop at 3:00. But he never

_____.

A: Hmm. What do you think _____ to him?

B: I don't know. I _____ for about 15 minutes and left without him.

A: Did you give him a call?

B: Yes, I _____ him, but he didn't pick up.

A: That's strange. I am going to send him an email.

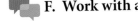 **F. Work with a partner. Practice the conversations in Activity E.**

GO ONLINE
to practice the
conversations

Step 2 SPEAK

A. Think of three experiences that have been interesting or important but also challenging to you. Write a sentence about each experience.

1. _____

2. _____

3. _____

Word Partners

give a presentation

give a talk

give a speech

give an exam

give an assignment

GO ONLINE
to practice
word partners

Speaking Skill

Follow-up questions

In conversations, listeners often use short questions to get more information on what the speaker has said. Listen to the examples.

Speaker	Listener
I went to a concert last night.	*Did you enjoy it?*
I stayed up all night working on a project.	*Did you finish on time?*
My roommate came home really late.	*Were you worried?*

B. Choose one of the experiences you listed in Activity A. Answer the questions.

1. Describe the experience (include when and where).

_____

2. How did you feel about the experience before it happened?

_____

3. What happened to you because of the experience?

_____

C. Work with a partner. Use your notes in Activity B to discuss your experiences.

Last year I went surfing for the first time in Australia.

Were you nervous?

Not really. I was excited to go.

Speaking Task

Discussing challenges in college

1. Prepare for a conversation. What is one challenge you have faced in college? Complete the chart.

Challenge _____
Why was it challenging?
1. _____
2. _____
3. _____

2. Work in a small group. Take turns discussing your challenges in college. Ask three follow-up questions to get more information about each person's experience.

Step 3 REPORT

Review your conversations. Think about one challenge you heard about. Write two to three sentences about the challenge.

Challenge _____
Why was it challenging?
1. _____
2. _____
3. _____

Step 4 REFLECT

Checklist

Check (✓) the things you learned in Chapter 1.

○ I learned words and phrases for talking about challenges and experiences.

○ I understood a lecture about challenges and taking risks.

○ I had a conversation about challenges in college.

Discussion Question

Are challenges good for you? Why or why not?

CHAPTER 2 Can Art Improve a Person's Life?

- Use *will* and *might*
- Listen for follow-up comments
- Recognize contractions

- Listen for phrases that signal order
- Practice syllable stress
- Make suggestions for an arts and culture project on campus

▲ VOCABULARY ▶ Oxford 2000 ✐ words to talk about art and leisure

Learn Words

🔊 **A. Label each picture with the correct word. Then listen and repeat the words and phrases.**

art	artist	concert	design	festival	gallery	museum	musician

1.
an art _____gallery_____

2.
an interesting _____

3.
a popular _____

4.
an outdoor _____

5.
a food and culture _____

6.
modern _____

7.
go to a(n) _____

8.
a famous _____

Grammar Note

will and *might*

🔊 Speakers use *will/won't* (or *'ll* in contracted form) to make predictions about the future. They also use *will/won't* to discuss decisions, promises, and offers. Speakers use *might/might not* when they are not sure about their predictions. Listen to the examples.

It*'ll* be sunny tomorrow. → future prediction

I*'ll* take you to the festival. → an offer

I **will** have the chicken curry, please. → a decision

I **won't** be home late. → a promise

She **might** join us this evening. She is not sure. → future possibility

🔊 **B. Listen and match the questions and answers.**

1. Which musician will play at the concert next month? __c__

2. What would you like, sir? _____

3. Are tickets to the concert sold out? _____

4. What's the weather forecast like? _____

5. Will you be finished by Saturday? _____

6. Where are you going after class? _____

a. I'll have the fish, please.

b. It'll be cold and rainy tomorrow.

c. ~~Somebody famous, I think.~~

d. I think I might finish on Sunday.

e. I might go to the library.

f. I'll sell you my ticket if you need one.

C. Complete each sentence with *might* or *will*.

1. He is not certain about the weather, but he said it _____ *might* _____ rain.

2. I _____ go with you if you need help.

3. I don't know what I am doing tomorrow. I _____ go shopping.

4. My friend _____ be here in exactly 20 minutes. Then we _____ leave.

D. Read each sentence. Check the meaning of *will*.

1. I'll finish cleaning if you have to go. ☑ offer   ☐ decision

2. I'll buy it for you. Don't worry. ☐ promise   ☐ prediction

3. It'll be a great performance. ☐ promise   ☐ prediction

4. I'll help you carry the heavy box. ☐ decision   ☐ offer

Learn Phrases

A. Match each phrase to the correct picture. Then listen and repeat.

do some sightseeing	learn about photography
experience a new culture	see a live performance
get tickets to a concert	study design
go to an art exhibition	take a class in painting

1.

2.

3.

4.

5.

6.

7.

8.

B. Listen to the speakers. Circle the phrase that completes each sentence.

1. The speaker says that the concert — (*is free.*)   *is famous.*

2. The speaker might — *visit an art gallery.*   *go sightseeing outside of the city.*

3. The speaker might — *go to a park.*   *visit an art exhibition.*

4. The speaker plans — *to do some sightseeing.*   *not to do some sightseeing.*

5. The speaker — *likes the design.*   *painted the design.*

6. The speaker is — *a great artist.*   *taking a class in painting.*

C. Match the questions and answers. Then ask and answer the questions with a partner.

1. Do you like modern art? __b__

2. Who is that? _____

3. Did you get tickets to the concert? _____

4. Are you going to study art and design? _____

5. Did you see the live performance? _____

a. She's a popular artist in Germany.

b. ~~Not really. I never understand it.~~

c. No, I plan to study animation.

d. No, I didn't. They were sold out.

e. Yes, it was great.

D. Think of a city you know. Where can you do the activities in the box? Complete the chart.

go to a food and culture festival	see modern art
go to a music festival	stay in a hostel
go to an art gallery	stay in a hotel
go to an outdoor concert	visit a museum
see a live performance	

In the city	Outside of the city

E. Work in a small group. Take turns describing some of the things in Activity D that you like to do.

GO ONLINE
for more
practice

Vocabulary   35

CONVERSATION

A. Listen to the conversation. Circle the phrases that describe Anna's plans.

go sightseeing   *stay in hotels*   *study in London*   *take a trip into the countryside*

B. Listen to the conversation again. Circle the correct phrase to complete each sentence.

1. Anna is   *studying art and design.*   *studying modern art.*
2. Brad   *wants to go to London.*   *has been to London.*
3. Anna is going to stay in   *a hotel.*   *a hostel.*

Listening Strategy

Listening for follow-up comments

Follow-up comments show interest or understanding. Speakers often use *that sounds* + adjective or *that sounds* + adjective + noun in follow-up comments. Listen to the examples.

> A: *I'm going to a see a live performance tonight.*
> B: **That sounds** <u>fun</u>.

> A: *I'm going to discuss my grade with the professor.*
> B: **That sounds** <u>like a good idea</u>.

GO ONLINE
for more
practice

C. Listen to part of the conversation again. Complete the comments with the phrases from the box.

that sounds cool	that sounds like fun	that'll be interesting

1. Brad: There's so much to see.

   Anna: _____.

2. Anna: I plan to visit the city's art galleries and museums every chance I get.

   Brad: _____.

3. Anna: I hear there are a lot of famous musicians coming there this summer.

   Brad: Yeah, _____.

D. Listen to part of the conversation again. Circle the follow-up comments you hear.

absolutely   *exactly*   *great point*   *that sounds good*   *true*

Contractions

🔊 A contraction combines two words into one. For instance, speakers often change *I will* to *I'll* in conversation.

That **will** be amazing. → That**'ll** be amazing.

She **will** help you out. → She**'ll** help you out.

I will not becomes *I won't* in conversation.

I **will not** have time. → I **won't** have time.

🔊 **E. Listen and complete the sentences. Then listen again and check your answers.**

1. _____*That'll*_____ be a lot of fun.

2. _____ arrive later.

3. _____ not going to buy tickets.

4. _____ already left.

5. _____ going to Boston in May.

6. _____ like to go sightseeing.

F. Write the underlined words in each sentence as a contraction.

1. <u>They are</u> taking a class in painting. _____*They're*_____

2. <u>They would</u> like to go back next month. _____

3. <u>It will</u> be cloudy tomorrow. _____

4. <u>They are</u> going to visit the art gallery. _____

5. She <u>does not</u> like traditional dance. _____

6. He <u>will not</u> be here tonight. _____

7. <u>They have</u> seen the performance. _____

8. They <u>did not</u> meet the artist. _____

🔊 **G. Listen to each speaker. Complete each sentence with the contraction you hear.**

1. Shao-Lin _____*isn't*_____ interested in art.

2. _____ planning to take a trip this weekend.

3. _____ finish by the end of the week.

4. _____ like to make a reservation, please.

5. He _____ work this morning.

6. She _____ do it.

Chant

GO ONLINE for the Chapter 2 Vocabulary and Grammar Chant

ACADEMIC LISTENING

💬 **A. Check the items that interest you. Share your answers with a partner.**

☐ traditional art   ☐ fashion design

☐ modern dance   ☐ traditional architecture

☐ classical music   ☐ animation

☐ painting   ☐ industrial design

🔊 **B. Listen to the talk about community arts. Mark each statement as *T* (true) or *F* (false).**

1. _____ The artists and local community worked together on the art project.

2. _____ The speaker helped build new buildings.

3. _____ People came to see the art project.

4. _____ The art project has been good for the local people.

🔊 **C. Listen to the talk again. Match the first part of each sentence with the second part.**

1. Community arts is _____

2. My friend wanted _____

3. Many people there wanted to paint _____

4. Tourists began _____

5. More money _____

a. to paint older buildings in his community.

b. is now coming into the community.

c. when professional artists work with local people to create art in their community.

d. traditional designs.

e. coming, too.

Listening Strategy

Listening for phrases that signal order

🔊 Speakers use sequence phrases to help listeners follow the order of events. Listen to some examples.

At the start of the day, *I visited the museum.*

Later, *I did some sightseeing around the city.*

At the end of the day, *I had a delicious meal at a famous restaurant.*

GO ONLINE
for more
practice

D. Number the statements in the correct order.

_____ Finally, I began attending classes in the fall.

_____ First, I applied to the program in the spring.

_____ Next I signed up for classes.

_____ Then I received an acceptance letter in the mail.

E. Listen to part of the talk again. Complete each sentence with a word or phrase from the box. You will not use all of the words.

| After that | At the end | Finally | First | Later on | Then | To start |

1. _____, we decided to raise money online.

2. _____ we started talking to people in the community.

3. _____, each day we worked with people in the community to paint buildings.

4. _____ of the project, the neighborhood looked beautiful.

F. Think of a project you worked on in the past. Some ideas are listed in the box. Write notes about the project.

an art project for a class	a project for a class
a community project	a project as an employee
a group project for a class	a project as a volunteer
an online project	a project in your home

1. What was the project/assignment? _____

2. How did you start it? _____

3. How did you finish it? _____

4. What was the result? _____

Discuss the Ideas

G. Look at your notes in Activity F. Discuss your project with a partner.

▲▲▲ SPEAKING

Speaking Task Making suggestions for an arts and culture project on campus

Step 1 PREPARE

Pronunciation Skill

Syllable stress

◀)) A stressed syllable in a word is usually longer, louder, and easier to hear. Stressing the correct syllable in a word can help listeners understand what you are saying. Listen to the examples.

Two-syllable nouns and adjectives often stress the first part of a word.

*I liked the web **plat**form.*

Compound nouns also often stress the first part of a word.

*You used all the **tooth**paste.*

GO ONLINE
for more
practice

◀)) **A. Underline the stressed syllable in each word. Then listen and check your answers.**

1. notebook
2. bathroom
3. breakfast
4. market
5. shower
6. table
7. nickname
8. workplace

◀)) **B. Listen and repeat.**

1. The artwork was beautiful.
2. I finally finished the project.
3. Football is one of my favorite sports.
4. I would love to go sightseeing.
5. There is an outdoor music festival this Saturday.
6. She already bought a ticket.
7. The building looked great.
8. I try to avoid danger.

C. Listen. Complete the conversation with the words you hear.

A: What did you think of the _____ student _____ art and design exhibition
   last week?

B: I thought it was nice. It's cool to see different types of art that students do
   on _____.

A: Yeah. And some _____ spent a lot of time on their projects.

B: There was one _____ that showed student _____.
   It was excellent.

A: I saw that section, but I really liked the design section. There were interesting designs
   for shoes, sunglasses, and watches. I even saw one for a _____. It
   looked very cool.

B: I hope to _____ my own work in next year's exhibition.

GO ONLINE
to practice the
conversation

D. Work with a partner. Practice the conversation in Activity C.

E. Complete the sentences with the words from the box. Then listen and check
   your answers.

airport	awesome	backpack	careful	concert
photo	schedule	snowstorm	whiteboard	~~window~~

1. Could you open the _____ window _____?

2. The instructors wrote the homework on the _____.

3. I'll print your _____ for you so you know when your classes start.

4. There was a _____ last night. The college canceled all classes.

5. I'll print the _____ of you and me and give it to you the next time we
   meet.

6. The musical was _____. I really enjoyed it.

7. Please be _____. The roads are icy today.

8. I usually carry everything in my _____.

9. They might go to the _____. Their favorite band is playing.

10. It takes about two hours to get to the _____. When is your flight?

Step 2 SPEAK

A. What arts, music, and cultural events take place on your campus? What are some events that your campus does not have? Complete the chart.

Events on campus	Events not on campus

B. Share your notes in Activity A with a partner.

Speaking Skill

Making suggestions

 Speakers use suggestions to offer ideas or give advice. There are several phrases you can use to make suggestions. Listen to the examples.

A: **You should** visit the art gallery downtown. B: That sounds like fun.

A: **Why don't you** study in the library? B: That sounds like a good place to go.

A: **You might want to** talk to the professor. B: Good idea.

C. Underline the statements that are suggestions. Then listen to the conversation.

A: I'd like to start an arts and culture club on campus for international students. How can I get started?

B: You should fill out a student club application form first. On the application, you should try to explain the kinds of activities the club will do.

A: Great. I'll do that. Is there anything else?

B: You might also want to provide lots of details on future club events.

A: Oh, OK. That's no problem.

B: There's just one more thing. After you finish your application, why don't you apply for funding with the Student Office? The Student Office gives student clubs on campus money for their events.

A: That's good to know. I'll definitely do that. Thank you.

D. Work with a partner. Practice the conversation in Activity C.

E. Work with a partner. Suggest a campus event or place to visit to your partner.

> You should see a performance at the art center.

> That sounds fun.

Speaking Task

Making suggestions for an arts and culture project on campus

1. Work with a partner. Choose a project that you want to start on your campus. Then tell your partner what you chose. Some ideas are listed.

> an art project to improve a campus building
>
> an international food festival
>
> a music festival
>
> an outdoor art exhibition
>
> a student-run magazine
>
> a student talent show

2. How can you start the project you chose? Write notes on the order of things you need to do.

First, _____.

Then _____.

After that, _____.

Finally, _____.

3. Work with your partner. Describe how you will start the project you chose. Use your notes.

Step 3 REPORT

A. Review your conversations. Write about your partner's project.

B. Work with a new partner. Share the two projects that you discussed.

Step 4 REFLECT

Checklist

Check (✓) the things you learned in Chapter 2.

○ I learned words and phrases about art.

○ I listened for words and phrases that signal order.

○ I understood a speaker discuss a community arts project.

Discussion Question

How do you think art can improve a community?

CHAPTER 3

How Important Is Work Experience?

- Use past simple and present perfect
- Listen for past simple and present perfect
- Recognize contractions with *has/have*

- Listen for chunking
- Practice verb reductions for *wh-* questions
- Discuss work experience

▲ VOCABULARY ▶ Oxford 2000 ✎ words to talk about work experience

Learn Words

🔊 **A. Label each picture with the correct word(s). Then listen and repeat the words and phrases.**

| apply for | be part of | earn | meetings | prepare | train | work in | ~~work with~~ |

1.

work with technology

2.

go to _____

3.

_____ a salary

4.

_____ new staff

5.

_____ a team

6.

_____ an office

7.

_____ a report

8.
_____ an internship

Grammar Note

Past simple and present perfect

Speakers often use the present perfect tense (*has/have* + past participle) to ask questions about past experiences. For the present perfect tense, speakers often use *ever* in questions to mean "at some time" and *never* in answers to mean at "no time up to now." Listen to the examples.

A: Have you **ever** been to Spain?   B: Yes, I have.   No, I haven't.

A: Have you **ever** met a famous musician?   B: No, I've never met a famous musician.

Speakers often use past simple questions to ask follow-up questions about the experience. Listen to the example.

A: Have you ever been to Guam?   B: Yes, I have.

A: When did you go?   B: I went there last year.

B. Listen to the pairs of sentences and write the correct verb form in each blank.

1. He has never _____*given*_____ a presentation.   He didn't _____ a chance to do it in high school.

2. She's _____ the fish.   She hasn't _____ the lamb.

3. I've _____ there before.   It _____ delicious.

4. I have never _____ surfing.   I _____ to do it last summer but didn't have time.

5. They've _____ a live performance.   They _____ one at the music festival last summer.

6. I have _____ in an office.   I _____ an internship before that.

C. Listen and match the questions and responses.

1. Have you ever lived abroad? ___*d*___

2. Have you ever given a class presentation? _____

3. Have you ever trained someone for a job? _____

4. Have you ever been part of a team? _____

5. Have you ever worked in an office? _____

6. Have you ever prepared a report for a job? _____

a. Yes, I have. I trained an intern last year.

b. No, I've never been part of one.

c. Yes, I have. I prepared a sales report for my team last month.

d. ~~Yes, I have. I lived in Brazil for three years.~~

e. No, I haven't.

f. Yes, I have.

D. Work with a partner. Ask and answer the questions in Activity C.

Learn Phrases

A. Match each phrase to the correct picture. Then listen and repeat.

choose a career in education	go on a job interview
commute to work	have a part-time job at the mall
deal with customers	work for a construction company
get a degree in engineering	write a resume

1.

2.

3.

4.

5.

6.

7.

8.

B. Listen to the speakers. Circle the phrase that completes each sentence.

1. The internship   *does not pay a monthly salary.*   *pays a small monthly salary.*

2. The speaker   *trained the new staff.*   *received training at the company.*

3. The speaker   *likes dealing with customers.*   *doesn't like dealing with customers.*

4. The speaker's problem is that   *she needs a resume.*   *she has no work experience.*

5. The speaker believes   *she will get the job.*   *it will be hard for her to get the job.*

 C. Listen and complete the sentences. Then listen again and repeat.

1. I'd like to work for a _____technology_____ company.

2. I chose to get a degree in _____.

3. I have _____ gone a job interview.

4. Dealing with customers is _____ in my opinion.

5. I _____ to work in teams.

 D. Rewrite the statements in Activity C to make them true for you. Then share your answers with a partner.

E. What are the most important items on a resume in your opinion? Rank the items (1 = most important, 5 = least important).

_____ work experience   _____ school grades

_____ education   _____ internship experience

_____ volunteer experience

F. Work with a partner. Ask and answer present perfect questions using the words from the box.

Question	Verb	Phrase
Have you ever	written dealt worked had gone	a part-time job? with customers? a resume? for a construction company? on a job interview?

G. Work in a small group. Discuss the questions.

1. What company would you like to do an internship with? Why?

2. What kind of work experience would you like to get?

3. Will you do an internship before you graduate? Why or why not?

GO ONLINE
for more
practice

▲▲ LISTENING

CONVERSATION

🔊 **A. Listen to the conversation between Ayman and Tian. Circle the name of the person each statement is true for.**

1. got a job after graduation   *Ayman*   *Tian*

2. gives advice about getting a job   *Ayman*   *Tian*

3. wants to work for a technology company   *Ayman*   *Tian*

🔊 **B. Listen to the conversation again. Circle the correct answers.**

1. Tian   *works with technology.*   *manages a team.*

2. Ayman   *has work experience in a*   *doesn't have work experience in a*
                 company.   *company.*

3. Tian suggests   *getting a part-time job.*   *applying for an internship.*

Listening Strategy

Listening for past simple and present perfect

🔊 Sometimes it can be difficult to hear the difference between past simple and present perfect. Past simple often uses past time markers, such as *yesterday, last,* and *ago,* but the present perfect does not. Listen to the examples.

Present perfect	*Have you ever been to Sumatra?*
	I haven't been there.
Past simple	*Did you like the lecture yesterday?*
	I enjoyed it.

GO ONLINE
for more
practice

🔊 **C. Listen to each statement. Circle *past simple* or *present perfect*.**

1. past simple   present perfect   2. past simple   present perfect

3. past simple   present perfect   4. past simple   present perfect

5. past simple   present perfect   6. past simple   present perfect

🔊 **D. Listen the conversation and fill in the blanks.**

A: Have you ever _____ an internship?

B: Yes, I _____.

A: When _____ you do it?

B: I _____ it last summer.

Contractions with *has/have*

🔊 When speakers use the present perfect tense, they often combine *has/have* with the subject of the sentence.

He **has** done it before. → He**'s** done it before.

We **have** been working all day. → We**'ve** been working all day.

🔊 **E. Listen and complete the sentences. Then listen again and repeat.**

1. _____I've_____ never gone skydiving.

2. _____ been there three times.

3. _____ seen it.

4. _____ had an internship.

5. No, they _____ written a resume yet.

6. _____ eaten it.

7. _____ driven the truck.

🔊 **F. Listen to each sentence. Circle the correct auxiliary verb that you hear. Then listen again and repeat.**

1. hasn't   (isn't)

2. has   is

3. has   is

4. has   is

5. has   is

6. hasn't   isn't

🔊 **G. Listen and fill in the blanks.**

1. _____Did_____ you _____ downtown last night?

2. _____ going tomorrow night.

3. _____ done it twice.

4. _____ prepared a report on the data.

5. He _____ a presentation yesterday.

6. _____ never _____ a resume.

Chant

GO ONLINE for the Chapter 3 Vocabulary and Grammar Chant

A. Work in a small group. Discuss the good and bad points of doing an internship. Fill in the table with your ideas.

Good points of doing an internship	Bad points of doing an internship
1. get work experience	1. work long hours
2.	2.
3.	3.

B. Work in a small group. Discuss the questions.

Should college students do an internship before graduating? Why or why not?

 C. Listen to the first part of the talk. Circle the correct answers.

1. The talk is at a   *career fair.*   *company.*   *news organization.*

2. Most students in the crowd   *have little work experience.*   *have a lot of work experience.*

3. The speaker says an   *will help students find a job.* *will help students earn a high*
   internship   *salary.*

D. Listen to the whole talk. Write down reasons the speakers give for doing an internship.

Moderator	Edward	Tina

E. Share your answers in Activity D with a partner.

Listening Strategy

Listening for chunking

 Chunking is when speakers combine words into a group. Chunking helps speakers stress important ideas and thoughts. Listen to the examples.

Work experience will help you get a job after you graduate.

Work experience / will help you get a job / after you graduate.

GO ONLINE
for more
practice

F. Listen and write a slash (/) at each break.

1. I work as an intern at a bank.

2. I think all students should try to find an internship.

3. Actually, I've learned that business really isn't right for me.

4. I hope to get a job after I graduate.

5. You might want to find an internship that pays well.

6. I suggest that all of you here use this opportunity to talk to companies about an internship.

G. Listen to part of the talk again. Write a slash (/) at each break.

Hello. I work in an office downtown for *City News*. I'm getting a degree in journalism and hope to work as a journalist after I graduate. And I believe that this internship experience will help me to get a job. Like Edward, I also earn a nice monthly salary, and that's helpful because I'm still a student. So, when you're looking for an internship, you might want to find one that pays well.

H. Read each sentence. Think about where the breaks will be. Then listen and check your answers.

1. You should really try to get some work experience.

2. Have you ever eaten at the restaurant on campus?

3. Do you have any work experience on your resume?

4. What type of company do you work for?

5. She really likes working with data.

6. I chose a career in business management.

I. Work with a partner. Ask and answer the questions.

Partner A	Partner B
1. What is the main topic of the talk?	2. What kind of company is Edward working for?
3. What kind of company is Tina working for?	4. Does Edward want a job in business after graduation?
5. Does Tina want to become a journalist after graduation?	6. What the does the speaker recommend to all students?

SPEAKING

Speaking Task Discussing work experience

Step 1 PREPARE

Pronunciation Skill

Verb reductions for *wh-* questions

When speakers ask *wh-* questions, the auxiliary verb is often reduced. Listen to the examples.

What **did** you do yesterday? → What**'d** you do yesterday?

Who **are** you going with? → Who**'re** you going with?

Where **have** you been? → Where**'ve** you been?

GO ONLINE
for more practice

A. Listen and repeat.

1. Where did they meet?

2. What did she do?

3. Who is he going to see?

4. Who is visiting?

5. When are you moving?

6. What is it for?

7. Where will you buy it?

8. Where have you been?

B. Match the full and reduced forms. Then listen and check your answers.

1. What is he doing? ___b___   a. Where'll

2. Where will you go? _____   b. ~~What's~~

3. When is it going to happen? _____   c. What'd

4. What did you do? _____   d. When's

5. Where have you gone? _____   e. Where'd

6. Where did you go? _____   f. Where've

7. When will you visit? _____   g. What've

8. What have they done? _____   h. When'll

C. Listen. Complete the interviews with the words you hear.

1. A: _____Have you had_____ any work experience?

   B: Yes, I've worked for a computer software company.

   A: What _____ at the company?

   B: Well, I worked with a lot of new technology. I also trained staff to use new technology and computer software.

   A: That's great. And why _____ a career in computer engineering?

   B: I like working with computers and being a part of teams that solve difficult problems.

   A: I see. Well, thank you for coming in. _____ in touch with you very soon.

   B: Thank you very much. I look forward to hearing from you.

2. A: OK, I was also looking over your resume. It says you _____ an internship?

   B: Yes, that's right. When I was student, I had an internship.

   A: What _____ for your internship?

   B: I was part of a sales team. I usually had to deal with customers, so I sold products and helped customers if they had problems using the products.

   A: Why _____ for a job with our company?

   B: I like the products that this company sells, and I think that working for this company is a great opportunity.

   A: OK. Thank you for your interest in our company. It _____ very nice talking with you.

   B: Thank you. It's been very nice talking with you.

GO ONLINE
to practice the conversations

D. Work with a partner. Practice the interview questions and answers in Activity C.

E. Work with a partner. Ask and answer the questions. Use reduced forms.

1. What did you do yesterday?

2. Where did you go last weekend?

3. Where will you go for your next vacation?

> What'd you do yesterday?

> I worked out at the gym.

Step 2 SPEAK

A. Write about some of your work and school experience. Some examples are given in the box.

analyzed data	taken a math class
dealt with customers	trained staff
done web design	used presentation software
given presentations	worked in teams
had a part-time job	worked on a class project
taken a business class	written reports

1. _____

2. _____

3. _____

Word Partners

apply for an internship

apply for a job

apply for a scholarship / program

apply for a passport

apply for a credit card

GO ONLINE
to practice
word partners

Speaking Skill

Asking for and giving advice

 In conversations, speakers sometimes ask for advice. There are several phrases that you can use to ask for and give advice. Listen to the examples.

What do you **think I should do**?	You **should** get a part-time job.
What do you **suggest**?	**Why don't you** learn a foreign language?
What do you **recommend**?	**You might want to** take classes in business.

 B. Complete each sentence to give advice. Then discuss your responses with a partner.

1. Where should I go if I visit your hometown?

You should _____.

2. What advice do you have for doing well in this class?

You might want to _____.

3. What restaurant do you recommend near campus?

Why don't you _____?

4. Where is a good place to meet new people?

You should _____.

C. Work with a partner. Take turns asking and answering the questions in Activity B.

Speaking Task

Discussing work experience

1. Take notes about your dream job in the chart.

What is your dream job?	Why is it your dream job?

2. Work with a partner. Discuss your notes in the chart. Does your work and school experience match the career you want?

3. Work in a small group. Ask for advice on getting work experience.

4. Work in a different small group. Make suggestions to help people find their dream jobs.

Step 3 REPORT

Review your conversations. Write down three of the suggestions you heard. Then answer the questions with a partner.

Suggestions
1. _____
2. _____
3. _____

1. Was the advice you heard helpful?

2. Do you think that you will follow any of the advice that you received? Why or why not?

Step 4 REFLECT

Checklist

Check (✓) the things you learned in Chapter 3.

○ I learned words and phrases for talking about work experience.

○ I understood a talk about internships.

○ I had a conversation about work experience.

Discussion Question

How important is work experience?

Look at the word bank for Unit 1. Check (✓) the words you know. Circle the words you want to learn better.

OXFORD 2000 ⚷

Adjectives	Nouns			Verbs	
foreign	art	design	lesson	apply	live
high	artist	education	meeting	avoid	move
interesting	business	exam	mountain	choose	prepare
long	career	experience	museum	climb	run
married	challenge	festival	musician	deal	take
new	class	food	painting	experience	train
popular	company	grade	race	face	try
	competition	home	ticket	get	visit
	computer	instrument	time	give	work
	concert	interview	top	have	write
	customer	job	work	learn	
	danger	language			

PRACTICE WITH THE OXFORD 2000 ⚷

A. Use the chart. Match adjectives with nouns.

1. _____an interesting job_____   2. _____

3. _____   4. _____

5. _____   6. _____

B. Use the chart. Match verbs with nouns.

1. _____prepare for an exam_____   2. _____

3. _____   4. _____

5. _____   6. _____

C. Use the chart. Match verbs with adjective noun partners.

1. _____try foreign food_____   2. _____

3. _____   4. _____

5. _____   6. _____

UNIT 2 Food

CHAPTER 4 How Much Cooking Do You Do?

▲ **VOCABULARY**
- Oxford 2000 🔑 words to talk about cooking

▲▲ **LISTENING**
- Listening for descriptions of words
- Listening for caveats

▲▲▲ **SPEAKING**
- Practicing *be* verbs in passive statements
- Describing a dish from your country

CHAPTER 5 How Do Eating Habits Differ?

▲ **VOCABULARY**
- Oxford 2000 🔑 words to talk about eating habits and customs

▲▲ **LISTENING**
- Listening for supporting information
- Listening for contrasts

▲▲▲ **SPEAKING**
- Practicing intonation in direct and indirect questions
- Surveying eating habits

CHAPTER 6 How Well Does Food Travel?

▲ **VOCABULARY**
- Oxford 2000 🔑 words to talk about food production

▲▲ **LISTENING**
- Listening for key words
- Listening for time markers

▲▲▲ **SPEAKING**
- Practicing adverb stress
- Leading a group discussion

UNIT WRAP UP Extend Your Skills

- Use simple passive
- Listen for descriptions of words
- Recognize vowel-vowel linking

- Listen for caveats
- Practice *be* verbs in passive statements
- Describe a dish from your country

▲ VOCABULARY ► Oxford 2000 ♪ words to talk about cooking

Learn Words

🔊 **A. Label each picture with the correct word. Then listen and repeat the words.**

| bitter | ~~boiled~~ | fried | salty | sour | spicy | steamed | sweet |

1.

boiled

2.

_____

3.

_____

4.

_____

5.

_____

6.

_____

7.
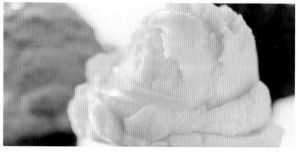
_____

8.

_____

Simple passive

🔊 Speakers use the passive voice to focus on the person or thing that an action happens to and not the person or thing doing it. Speakers form simple passive statements with the verb *to be* and the past participle (e.g., *eaten, seen*). Listen to the examples.

Active	**Passive**
They baked it this morning.	*It was baked this morning.*

🔊 In passive sentences, speakers often use the prepositions *by* to describe who does an action and *at* to describe where an action happens. Listen to the examples.

	Active	**Passive**
Present:	*The shop sells many products.*	*Many products are sold at the shop.*
Past:	*Our team completed the project.*	*The project was completed by our team.*

🔊 **B. Complete each sentence using the correct form of the verb in parentheses. Then listen and check your answers.**

1. New ideas (be exchange) _____*are exchanged*_____ at the conference every year.

2. Large pans (be use) _____ for baking at our restaurant.

3. The cake (not be make) _____ yesterday.

4. The product (be deliver) _____ by a driver later today.

5. Cheese and meat (be sell) _____ at the market on Saturdays.

6. Dishes (not be cook) _____ with vegetable oil at our restaurant.

C. Change each active sentence to a passive sentence.

1. The driver delivers the food.

*The food is delivered by the driver.*_____

2. Elementary school students play the game.

_____

3. The company did not sell the products last year.

_____

4. The factory produces three types of cars.

_____

5. A famous chef prepared the dish.

_____

6. The bakers did not finish the cakes on time.

_____

Learn Phrases

🔊 **A. Match each phrase to the correct picture. Then listen and repeat.**

be baked in an oven	cut into small pieces
be made with chili peppers	fry in vegetable oil
be served with	mix the ingredients together
cook for a long time	put the meat in a large pan

1.

2.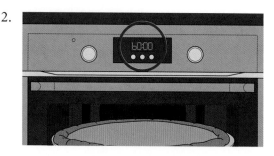

3.

4.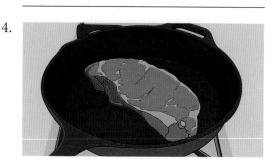

5.

6.

7.

8.

B. Listen to the speakers. Circle the correct answers.

1. This dish   *is spicy.*   (*isn't spicy.*)

2. The dish has   *a salty taste.*   *different flavors.*

3. The food   *was   wasn't*   served with bread and olives.

4. The vegetables   *are served fresh.*   *are cooked.*

5. The speaker   *dislikes   likes*   the dish with lemon.

6. The dish is   *too spicy   too salty*   for some people.

C. Place the words in the box in the correct columns in the chart.

| cake | chili peppers | fish sauce | garlic | lemon |

Tastes sweet	Tastes bitter	Tastes salty	Tastes sour	Tastes spicy

D. Work with a partner. Add foods to the chart in Activity C.

E. Work in a small group. Ask and answer the questions.

1. Who does most of the cooking in your family?

2. What is the spiciest dish you have tried? Was it good?

3. Do you enjoy cooking? Why or why not?

F. Complete the sentences. Then share your answers with a partner.

1. _____ is/are baked in an oven.

2. _____ is/are cooked for a long time.

3. _____ is/are fried in vegetable oil.

4. _____ is/are made with _____.

5. _____ is/are cut into small pieces when making _____.

Cookies are baked in an oven.   Risotto is made with rice.

GO ONLINE
for more
practice

▲▲ LISTENING

CONVERSATION

🔊 **A. Listen to the conversation. Circle the topics the speakers talk about.**

buying ingredients   *cooking at home*   *different flavors*   *eating at a restaurant*

🔊 **B. Listen to the conversation again. Mark *T* (true) or *F* (false) for each statement.**

1. _____ The woman plans to cook at home.

2. _____ The speakers talk about how to make pad thai.

3. _____ Pad thai has several different flavors.

Listening Strategy

Listening for descriptions of words

🔊 Speakers often give descriptions of new or uncommon words. Listening for descriptions can help you learn and understand new words. Speakers use different strategies for describing words. Listen to the examples.

Description strategy

Purpose: *A baking pan is used for making cakes.*

Examples: *Kitchenware is pots, pans, and other items in the kitchen.*

Senses: *The sauce smells delicious but tastes a little too salty.*

GO ONLINE
for more
practice

C. Read each statement. Write *purpose, senses,* or *examples*.

_____ 1. It's red and has a sweet smell.

_____ 2. They often include ketchup, mustard, salt, and pepper.

_____ 3. People put books on them.

_____ 4. People often go there to exercise.

🔊 **D. Listen to part of the conversation. Circle all of the correct answers.**

1. Pad thai is made with   *steamed rice.   steamed noodles.   eggs.   garlic.   vegetables.*

2. Pad thai tastes   *sweet.   sour.   bitter.   salty.   spicy.*

Sounds of English

Recognizing vowel-vowel linking

🔊 When a word ends in a vowel sound and the next word begins with a vowel, speakers often make either a /y/ or a /w/ sound. Listen to the examples.

I am a waiter. → *I **(y)am** a waiter.*

Let's go out for dinner tonight. → *Let's go **(w)out** for dinner tonight.*

🔊 **E. Listen and repeat.**

1. We asked what time to come.

2. Who is it?

3. When can you do it?

4. Turn right and then go under the bridge.

5. Go inside and have a seat.

6. If you can stay out a little longer, we can finish the assignment.

7. Be on time for class in the future.

🔊 **F. Listen and circle whether you hear /y/ or /w/ between the underlined words.**

1. <u>He asked</u> where to go.   /y/   /w/

2. William wants to <u>try out</u> for the team.   /y/   /w/

3. She is <u>also in</u> the class.   /y/   /w/

4. The instructor told us to <u>do all</u> of the problems.   /y/   /w/

5. You can <u>see it</u> at night.   /y/   /w/

6. I was <u>too excited</u> about the trip. I couldn't sleep.   /y/   /w/

🔊 **G. Listen to each statement. Complete the statement with the words you hear.**

1. There's no _____ *way out* _____ of here.

2. I just want to _____ the bed for a while.

3. I plan to _____ over Europe this summer.

4. _____ I were late last time.

5. You work _____.

6. I _____ of the problems on the exam.

7. _____ an excellent cook.

Chant

GO ONLINE for the Chapter 4 Vocabulary and Grammar Chant

A. How difficult is it to make the foods shown? Rank them (most difficult = 1, least difficult = 5).

a cake

_____

fried rice

_____

chicken curry

_____

falafel

_____

pasta with tomato sauce

_____

B. Compare your answers in Activity A with a partner.

C. Listen to the cooking show. Circle the topics the speaker talks about.

baking turkey   *frying food in vegetable oil*   *making gravy*

Listening Strategy

Listening for caveats

A caveat is a warning or extra information about something. Speakers often use the word *though* when giving caveats. Listen to the example.

*The health food store has great products. It closes very early **though**.*

GO ONLINE
for more
practice

D. Match each statement to a caveat.

1. The food in the cafeteria is cheap. __b__
2. The class is really interesting. _____
3. The mall has a big sale tomorrow. _____
4. That movie is really funny. _____
5. I love playing baseball. _____

a. It starts early in the morning.

b. ~~It doesn't taste very good.~~

c. Tickets to the theater are expensive.

d. The stores will be really busy.

e. My friends don't play it.

E. Work with a partner. Practice saying the statements in Activity D using the word *though*.

> The food in the cafeteria is cheap.
> It doesn't taste very good though.

F. Match each statement to a caveat. Then listen to part of the cooking show again and check your answers.

1. Salt will give your turkey a nice flavor. _____

2. This is the best way to make a delicious turkey. _____

3. I have put a recipe for gravy that I like to use on our website. _____

a. There are many ways to make gravy though.

b. The turkey needs to cook for a long time though.

c. You don't want to use too much though.

G. Listen to the cooking show again. Ask and answer the questions with a partner.

Partner A	Partner B
1. How is turkey usually cooked?	2. What vegetables does the speaker use?
3. What does the speaker say not to use too much of?	4. How long does it take to bake a turkey?
5. What happens after the turkey is cooked?	6. What is turkey usually served with?

Discuss the Ideas

H. Work in a small group. Discuss the questions.

1. What kinds of herbs and spices are used in food in your country?

2. What are some popular dishes in your country?

3. What time do people normally eat their meals in your country?

SPEAKING

Speaking Task Describing a dish from your country

Step 1 PREPARE

Pronunciation Skill

be verbs in passive statements

🔊 In passive statements, speakers often stress the main verb of the sentence but do not stress forms of *be* (e.g., *am, is, are, was, were*). In negative statements, the word *not* is also unstressed. Listen to the examples.

*The assignment **is** done online.*

*The report **wasn't** completed.*

GO ONLINE for more practice

🔊 **A. Listen and repeat the statements.**

1. The email was sent by my assistant.

2. The class isn't scheduled on Tuesdays.

3. The package was delivered by the company.

4. Cars are built at the factory.

5. Flowers are planted at the park every spring.

6. Different herbs and spices are used in the dish.

7. The software program wasn't created by our team.

🔊 **B. Listen to each statement and circle the word you hear.**

1. Tickets   *are*   (*were*)   checked at the front gate.

2. The project   *isn't*   *wasn't*   finished on time.

3. The presentations   *are*   *were*   given at the main hall.

4. Fruits and vegetables   *are*   *were*   sold at the market.

5. The class   *isn't*   *wasn't*   canceled.

6. Three students   *are*   *were*   hired by the company.

7. It   *isn't*   *wasn't*   done there.

C. Listen. Complete the conversations with the words you hear.

1. A: Do you have any questions about the menu?

   B: Yes, _____ how is _____ the fish cooked?

   A: It's grilled, and _____ with delicious herbs and spices. It's one of my favorite _____ on the menu.

   B: That sounds delicious. Is it fresh?

   A: It _____ in this morning, so, yes, it's very fresh.

   B: That's great. I'll have the fish then, please.

   A: Great choice.

2. A: What does the grilled chicken come with?

   B: It _____ with steamed _____ and soup.

   A: OK. That sounds good.

   B: It's very good. And all of our vegetables _____ on local farms.

   A: I will get the grilled chicken, please. Could I also have a glass of water with my meal?

   B: Yes, of course. I'll _____ that right away.

   A: Thank you very much.

GO ONLINE to practice the conversations

D. Work with a partner. Practice the conversations in Activity C.

E. Work with a partner. Use the phrases in the box to make passive statements.

My car	is taught	in an envelope.
Reservations	wasn't hit	by the customers.
The class	were returned	at the hotel's website.
The letter	was mailed	by Professor Lawson once a week.
The broken items	are made	by the truck.

A. Think about a popular dish in your country. Check (✓) the statements that are true about the dish.

☐ It tastes sour.

☐ It takes a long time to cook.

☐ It is made with meat.

☐ It is served with vegetables.

Word Partners

fast food

food poisoning

fresh food

frozen food

grow food

health food

order food

store food

GO ONLINE
to practice
word partners

Speaking Skill

Describing words you don't know

When you do not know a word in English, you can describe the word to help the listener understand what you are talking about. There are different ways to describe words you don't know. Listen to the examples.

Example

Turkey—it's a type of bird.

Purpose

A rice cooker—it's a machine that is used to make rice.

Senses (how something looks, tastes, smells, sounds, or feels)

A chili pepper—it's red and tastes spicy.

B. Match the words and their descriptions.

1. watermelon _____

2. cheese _____

3. coffee _____

4. chocolate _____

a. It's usually sweet and dark brown.

b. Some people drink it in the morning or when they are tired.

c. It's mozzarella, Swiss, and cheddar. People put it on sandwiches.

d. It's large and heavy. It's green on the outside and red inside.

C. Work with a partner. Describe dishes you know about. Use the words in the box and your own ideas.

Examples	Senses		Purposes
fish	soft	bitter	used to make...
grows on trees	hard	salty	eaten with...
is meat	sour		cooked in...
is a fruit	sweet		
is made with fish			

Speaking Task

Describing a dish from your country

1. Think about a popular dish in your country. Take notes on the dish.

> **Dish name:** _____
>
> What is it made with? _____
> How is it cooked? _____
> What does it taste like?_____
> What does it look like? _____
> What is it served with? _____

2. Work in a small group. Take turns describing your dish. Takes notes on the dishes in the chart.

Classmate's name	Dish name	Notes

Step 3 REPORT

A. Review your notes. Answer the questions.

1. Which dishes have you heard of?

2. Which dishes do you want to try?

B. Work with a partner from another group. Use your notes to describe two different dishes to your partner.

Step 4 REFLECT

Checklist

Check (✓) the things you learned in Chapter 4.

○ I learned words and phrases for talking about cooking.

○ I understood a talk show about how to cook a turkey.

○ I described a popular dish in my country.

Discussion Question

How important is it for families to eat together?

CHAPTER 5

How Do Eating Habits Differ?

- Use indirect questions
- Listen for supporting information
- Reductions in indirect questions
- Listen for contrasts
- Practice intonation in direct and indirect questions
- Survey eating habits

▲ VOCABULARY ▶ Oxford 2000 ✿ words to talk about eating habits and customs

Learn Words

🔊 **A. Label each picture with the correct word. Then listen and repeat the words and phrases.**

| diet | help | leave | main | out | social | traditional | use |

1.

_____main_____ meal

2.

_____ chopsticks

3.

_____ a tip

4.

eat _____

5.

_____ yourself

6.

a vegetarian _____

7.

a(n) _____ recipe

8.

a(n) _____ event

Grammar Note

Indirect questions

Indirect questions are more polite or formal than direct questions. When an indirect question has a *yes/no* answer, the indirect question uses the word *if* and a positive statement. Listen to the examples.

Direct form	Indirect form + *if* + positive statement
Does your friend like sushi? →	*Do you know if your friend likes sushi?*
Has she been there before? →	*Do you have any idea if she has been there before?*
Is she from Kenya? →	*Can you tell me if she is from Kenya?*

B. Listen and complete the indirect questions. Then listen again and repeat the direct and indirect questions.

1. Is that a traditional recipe?

   Do you _____have_____ any idea if that is a traditional recipe?

2. Is the course full?

   Do you _____ if the course is full?

3. Does the dish come with beef?

   Could you _____ me if the dish comes with beef?

4. Do you like fried rice?

   I'd _____ to know if you like fried rice.

C. Check (✓) each correct question or statement.

1. [✓] Do you know if she is home?   [ ] Do you know she is home?

2. [ ] Do you have any idea if does she like it?   [ ] Do you have any idea if she likes it?

3. [ ] I'd like to know if it is healthy.   [ ] I'd like to know if it healthy is.

4. [ ] Do you know the professor is sick?   [ ] Do you know if the professor is sick?

D. Change the direct questions into indirect questions or statements using the phrases in parentheses. Then check your answers with a partner.

1. Is the restaurant open today? (Could you tell me)

2. Does Mia have a vegetarian diet? (Do you know)

3. Does your friend like sports? (Do you have any idea)

4. Have you ever been abroad? (I'd like to know)

Learn Phrases

🔊 **A. Match each phrase to the correct picture. Then listen and repeat.**

buy food from the grocery store	get together with friends and family
eat three meals a day	have a cup of coffee in the morning
eat with a fork and knife	choose fresh fruits and vegetables
get food delivered	try different types of food

1.

2.

3.

4.

5.

6.

7.

8.

B. Listen to the speakers. Write *T* (true) or *F* (false) for each statement.

1. ___F___ Lin likes to eat with her coworkers in their office.

2. _____ The speaker gets food delivered to her office.

3. _____ The main meal of the day for the speaker is lunch.

4. _____ The speaker is worried because there are no vegetarian dishes.

5. _____ The speaker can't pick her own fruit as often as she would like.

6. _____ The speaker thinks it is easy to learn cultural customs.

C. Check (✓) the items that are true for you. Then share your answers with a partner.

1. _____ I follow a vegetarian diet.

2. _____ I usually have a cup of coffee in the morning.

3. _____ I usually eat three meals a day.

4. _____ The main meal of the day for me is breakfast.

5. _____ I enjoy trying different types of food.

6. _____ I get food delivered to my home once a week.

7. _____ I usually eat my meals with a fork and knife.

D. Work in small group. Ask and answer the questions.

1. How often do people in your country eat out?

2. What types of restaurants do you eat out at?

3. Why do you think some people follow a vegetarian diet?

4. Where you live, what kinds of food can you get delivered to your home?

GO ONLINE
for more
practice

▲▲ LISTENING

CONVERSATION

🔊 **A. Listen to the survey. Circle the things the speakers talk about.**

dinner   *eating habits*   *eating out*   *snacks*

🔊 **B. Listen to the survey again. Write *T* (true) or *F* (false) for each statement.**

1. _____ The woman's main meal is breakfast.

2. _____ The woman usually eats dinner at home.

3. _____ The woman does not buy food at the grocery store.

GO ONLINE
for more
practice

Listening Strategy

Listening for supporting information

🔊 Listening for the main idea is important for understanding a conversation. Listening for supporting information related to the main idea can help improve your listening skills and give you more information. Listen to the examples.

Main thought	**Supporting information**
I enjoy many kinds of food.	*I like Italian, Indian, and Lebanese food.*

🔊 **C. Listen to the survey again. Write supporting information for each of the survey responses in the chart.**

	Supporting information
Main meal is breakfast	
Doesn't eat dinner at home	
Buying food	

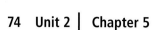 **D. Work with a partner. Share the supporting information you wrote in the chart in Activity C.**

Reductions in indirect questions

When speakers ask indirect questions quickly, they often link the word *if* with pronouns that follow it. For instance, *if she* sounds like "ifshi." Listen to the examples.

*Do you know **if he** goes there?* → *Do you know **ify** goes there?*

*Do you have any idea **if she** likes it?* → *Do you have any idea **ifshi** likes it?*

*Can you tell me **if it's** a good idea?* → *Can you tell me **ifits** a good idea?*

E. Listen and repeat.

1. Do you know if she's been there?

2. I'd like to know if we can buy tickets.

3. Could you tell if it is enough?

4. Do you have any idea if he finished on time?

5. I'd like to know if he is coming to the event.

6. Could you tell me if you are going to eat with us?

F. Listen and complete the questions with the words you hear.

1. Do you know _____*if it's*_____ at the library?

2. Could you tell me _____ giving us a test next week?

3. Do you have any idea _____ going to be nice tomorrow?

4. Do you know _____ interested in playing?

5. I'd like to know _____ tried it yet.

6. Can you tell me _____ seen the movie?

G. Work with a partner. Write down three things that you would like to know about your partner.

1. _____

2. _____

3. _____

H. Ask and answer indirect questions with your partner using what you wrote in Activity G. Use the phrases *I'd like to know* and *I was wondering*.

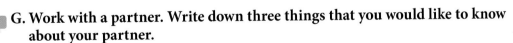

I'd like to know if you like to jog.

Chant

GO ONLINE for the Chapter 5 Vocabulary and Grammar Chant

ACADEMIC LISTENING

A. What is a family dinner usually like in your country? Write *T* (true) or *F* (false) for each statement.

1. _____ There are six or more different dishes.

2. _____ There are many rules for younger people to follow.

3. _____ People avoid talking during the meal.

4. _____ The oldest people get their food first.

5. _____ The meal is usually vegetarian.

6. _____ Meals are eaten with a fork and knife.

 B. Discuss your answers in Activity A with a partner.

C. Listen to the lecture. Circle the correct answers.

1. The speaker describes eating as   *a social event.*   *a way to try new foods.*

2. In South Korea, there are   *many cultural customs.*   *many rules for older people.*

3. In Italy, meals   *are usually short.*   *can take several hours.*

D. Listen to part of the lecture again. Circle the correct answers.

1. In South Korea, when younger people pass food to older people, they use
   one hand.   *two hands.*

2. In Italy, Sunday lunch allows people   *to share stories.*   *to get to know each other.*

3. There are   *many cultural customs for eating.*   *three customs followed by most people.*

Listening Strategy

Listening for contrasts

Speakers use contrasts to show how two things are different. To show a contrast, speakers will often use specific words to tell the listener that they are comparing two ideas. Listen to the examples.

The restaurant serves excellent food. **However**, *it is very expensive.*

The main meal is dinner here, **but** *the main meal in Spain is lunch.*

My school is really great, **although** *it is a little far from my home.*

GO ONLINE
for more
practice

E. Listen to each statement. Complete the statement with a word or phrase from the box. One word or phrase will be used twice.

although	but	even though	however

1. They really like Thai food, _____ but _____ they don't like the spicy dishes.

2. The class is useful. _____, it is difficult.

3. _____ he's 75 years old, he jogs every day.

4. She didn't finish _____ she had three days to do it.

5. The new gym in my apartment building is really nice, _____ I have to pay a fee to use it.

F. Work with a partner. Use *but* and *however* to contrast the sentences in the chart.

She loves playing hockey. I exercise every day. I left my house one hour ago. We lost the game. They worked very hard.	but however	They got a low grade on the project. I haven't lost weight. Our team was much better than the other team. I still arrived late. It's too hot for hockey where she lives.

G. Listen to the lecture again. Ask and answer the questions with a partner.

Partner A	Partner B
1. Why is eating often a social event?	2. How do younger people pass food in South Korea?
3. Why might vegetarians have difficulty in South Korea?	4. Which meal is an important tradition in Italy?
5. What does a long meal allow Italians to do?	6. What will the class learn about this semester?

Discuss the Ideas

H. Work in a small group. Discuss the questions.

1. What are some cultural rules when having food in your country?

2. Does having a four-hour lunch sound good to you? Why or why not?

3. How long is lunch in your country?

4. Do you know any cultural rules to follow when having food in other countries? Explain your answer.

Speaking Task Surveying eating habits

Step 1 PREPARE

Pronunciation Skill

GO ONLINE
for more
practice

Intonation in direct and indirect questions

When speakers ask direct *yes/no* questions, their intonation often rises at the end of the question. For indirect questions, intonation rises before the word *if* and at the end of the question. Listen to the examples.

Did he work on the project?   *Do you know if he worked on the project?*

Is the farmer's market open?   *Can you tell me if the farmer's market is open?*

A. Listen and repeat.

1. Is this shirt on sale?

2. Has she been to the new outdoor market?

3. Does the dish come with rice?

4. Does the store sell organic food?

5. Has everyone tried the baked fish?

6. Does healthy food help fight illness?

B. Listen and complete each statement with the word(s) you hear.

1. Can you tell _____ me _____ if this shirt is on sale?

2. Do you _____ if she's been to the new outdoor market?

3. Do you _____ if this dish comes with _____ ?

4. Do you have any _____ if the store sells organic _____ ?

5. I was _____ if everyone has tried the baked _____ .

6. I'd like to _____ if healthy food helps fight _____ .

C. Listen and match the questions and answers.

1. Do you know if the bus stops here? ___e___

2. Can you tell me if the library is open? _____

3. Do you have any idea if laptops are sold here?

_____

4. I was wondering if you are finished with the assignment. _____

5. I'd like to know if you bought the course textbook. _____

a. No, I'm borrowing a friend's book.

b. Actually, I just finished it last night.

c. No, we do not sell laptops here.

d. I think so. It usually closes late.

e. Yes, it stops here every 20 minutes.

D. Work with a partner. Practice asking and answering the questions in Activity C.

E. Listen. Complete the conversations with the words you hear.

1. A: Have you been to the new campus _____café_____ ?

   B: No, I _____. Do you know if it's any _____?

   A: No, but I heard that it's _____ cheap.

2. A: Do you have _____ idea if _____ is an app for dieting?

   B: Yeah, there is. I _____ one.

   A: Is it _____?

   B: No, it's free.

3. A: Hi, I was _____ where the computer lab is.

   B: Oh, it's on the _____ floor.

   A: Thank you. And do you have _____ idea if it has printers?

   B: Yes, it does, but you have to _____ for the paper.

4. A: Does _____ have any questions?

   B: Yes, do you know if the _____ has a website?

   A: That's a _____ question. Yes, there is a website for the class. It's on the syllabus.

   B: Do you know if we have to log in?

   A: Yes, you just log in _____ your student ID number.

F. Listen to the conversations in Activity E again. Mark ^ where you hear rising intonation in questions.

G. Work with a partner. Practice the conversations in Activity E.

H. Write three questions about the class, college, or city you are in now. Then ask and answer the questions with a partner.

1. Can you tell me if _____ ?

2. Do you know if _____ ?

3. Do you have any idea if _____ ?

GO ONLINE
to practice the
conversations

Word Partners

a delicious meal

a light meal

a late meal

a big meal

an expensive meal

GO ONLINE
to practice
word partners

A. Think about eating habits and customs in your country. Check (✓) the statements that are true in your country.

☐ People leave a tip for the server at a restaurant.

☐ Lunch is usually at noon.

☐ The oldest person usually pays for a meal at a restaurant.

☐ People often put a napkin in their lap when they eat.

☐ People usually eat with chopsticks.

Speaking Skill

Giving yourself time to think

When people are asked questions, they often need time to think. Using words or phrases such as *well* or *let's see* tells the other person that you are interested and thinking about your answer. Listen to the examples.

Let's see... *I guess breakfast is the biggest meal of the day for me.*

Well... *I usually eat three meals a day.*

B. Listen to the conversations. Complete the sentences with the words you hear.

1. A: About how many times a day do you eat meat?

   B: _____ me think about it. I guess I eat meat about twice a day.

2. A: Where do you usually buy food?

   B: That's a good _____. I get most of my food from the grocery store.

3. A: Do you know if you eat organic fruits and vegetables?

   B: I'm not _____. I don't actually check if fruits and vegetables are organic when I buy them.

4. A: Do you ever skip breakfast?

   B: You _____, I skip it almost every day.

C. Work with a partner. Practice the conversations in Activity B.

Speaking Task

Surveying eating habits

1. Survey a classmate on the questions in the chart. Imagine that you are surveying people who you do not know and use indirect questions to be more polite.

> Is your main meal of the day dinner?
>
> Do you eat three meals a day?
>
> Do you buy most of your food at a grocery store?
>
> Are there any rules or cultural customs when you eat?
>
> Do you usually eat alone?

2. Survey two more classmates on the questions in the chart.

Step 3 REPORT

A. Complete the chart about the survey you did.

Things that were the same for the people you talked to	
Things that were different for the people you talked to	
Things that were surprising or interesting	

B. Work with a partner. Share what you wrote in Activity A.

Step 4 REFLECT

Checklist

Check (✓) the things you learned in Chapter 5.

- ○ I learned words and phrases for talking about eating habits and customs.
- ○ I understood a talk about eating habits and customs.
- ○ I did a survey of eating habits.

Discussion Question

How important is it that families eat together? Why?

CHAPTER 6

How Well Does Food Travel?

- Use *so/such*
- Listen for key words
- Recognize consonant-vowel linking

- Listen for time markers
- Practice adverb stress
- Lead a group discussion

▲ VOCABULARY ▶ Oxford 2000 ✎ words to talk about food production

Learn Words

🔊 **A. Label each picture with the correct word. Then listen and repeat the words.**

grow	pack	pick	plant	prepare	produce	store	transport

1.
produce

2.

3.

4.

5.

6.

7.

8.

Grammar Note

so/such

🔊 Speakers use intensifiers to describe adjectives and to make them stronger. The intensifiers *so* and *such* make adjectives stronger but use different grammatical forms. *Such* is used with count, noncount, and plural nouns. Listen to the examples.

so + adjective

*They grow **so many** vegetables.*

*This assignment is **so boring**.*

such + adjective + noun

*Spencer prepared **such a big meal**.*   singular count noun

*I had **such a nice time** last night.*   singular noncount noun

*They are **such good friends**.*   plural noun

🔊 **B. Listen and repeat each statement.**

1. They transported the food so far.
2. Nora cooks such good meals.
3. I picked so many beans.
4. They are such good athletes.
5. They sent us such a nice card.
6. The trip was so long.
7. The gift was so big.
8. It was such an expensive house.

C. Complete each sentence with *so* or *such*.

1. I am _____ so _____ excited about my trip.

2. I am sorry. I am _____ tired right now.

3. You are _____ a smart person.

4. That was _____ a long game.

💬 **D. Complete the sentences with your own ideas. Then share your answers with a partner.**

1. I had such a good time _____.

2. _____ was so interesting in my opinion.

3. _____ is so boring to me.

4. The weather in _____ is so hot in the summer.

5. _____ is such an interesting movie.

6. _____ is such a hard job.

> I had such a good time on my vacation last summer.

Learn Phrases

A. Match each phrase to the correct picture. Then listen and repeat.

be grown on a farm	make a new discovery
pack a lunch	move from one continent to another
create a new dish	produce food products
feed a large city	transport goods by ship

1.

2.

3.

4.

5.

6.

7.

8.

B. Listen to the speakers. Circle the correct answers.

1. International trade has   *improved food quality.*   *changed what people eat.*

2. The speaker   *eats out for lunch.*   *packs a lunch.*

3. It will be cheaper to send the goods   *by ship.*   *by plane.*

4. Advanced machinery   *is used in cities.*   *helps feed cities.*

5. Less popular items are   *cheaper.*   *more expensive.*

6. The scientists   *didn't discover*   *discovered*   new plants on their trip.

C. Mark if the statements are true (*T*) or false (*F*) for you. Then share your opinions with a partner.

1. _____ Farming seems like an interesting job.

2. _____ I usually pack a lunch for myself at home.

3. _____ I live in a large city in my country.

4. _____ I usually buy food from the grocery store.

5. _____ I like to buy fruits and vegetables at a farmer's market.

D. Describe the process of food production. Number the statements in the correct order. Then share your answers with a partner.

_____ The seeds grow and produce fruits and vegetables.

_____ People buy the fruits and vegetables and prepare food with them at home.

_____ The fruits and vegetables are packed onto a truck.

_____ The farmer picks the fruits and vegetables.

_____ The fruits and vegetables are sold in a grocery store.

_____ The fruits and vegetables are transported to a grocery store.

___1___ A farmer plants seeds.

E. Work in a small group. Ask and answer the questions.

1. Are there any restaurants that you want to try? Explain your answer.

2. Where do you find reviews of restaurants?

3. Does your favorite restaurant prepare most of its food fresh?

GO ONLINE
for more
practice

▲▲ LISTENING

CONVERSATION

A. Listen to the conversation. Circle the correct answers.

1. The main topic of the conversation is   *farming.*   *a restaurant.*

2. The speakers will go to   *a farm*   *a restaurant*   together.

Listening Strategy

Listening for key words

Key words are the important words of a sentence that carry meaning. All of the underlined words in the examples below have meaning, but the other words do not. Speakers often stress or repeat the most important key words. Listen to the examples.

She goes to the **supermarket every week.**

The **bus took** *the* **long route** *to the* **game.**

GO ONLINE
for more practice

B. Underline key words in each statement. Then listen to the statements.

1. International trade has changed the way people eat around the world.

2. It has become such an important way to feed large cities and growing populations.

3. When different food products move from one continent to another, new ideas for dishes are often created.

C. Listen to part of the conversation. Write some of the key words you hear to complete the sentences.

1. Actually, I had _____ there last _____. It was so

   _____.

2. I'd love to go back. Huriya's right. Everything is prepared with _____

   _____ and herbs and spices.

3. They also sell pack _____ for takeout, too.

4. So they'll pack us a lunch made with _____ _____

   and _____, and we can eat in the park or on _____.

D. Listen to the conversation again. Mark *T* (true) or *F* (false) for each statement.

1. _____ Two of the speakers have been to the restaurant.

2. _____ Food at the restaurant comes from a farm.

3. _____ The restaurant sells pack lunches and other food products.

Sounds of English

Recognizing consonant-vowel linking

A consonant sound can move to the next word when it begins with a vowel. Listen to the examples.

You'll love it. → *You'll **lu-vit**.*

We're going to take a cab. → *We're gonna **tae-ka** cab.*

The instructor told us what was on the exam. → *The instructor **tol-dus** what **wa-son** the exam.*

E. Listen and repeat.

1. Is it time to go?

2. We have run out of food.

3. Tell us what your plans are for the weekend.

4. Could you turn on the TV?

5. It's such a nice setup.

6. I'm so sick of studying.

F. Listen and complete the statements with the phrases from the box.

heard of	keep it	~~lots of~~	put it	that's all	types of

1. We have _____ lots of _____ food in the fridge.

2. You can _____ if you want.

3. _____ the sugar we have.

4. We saw different _____ animals on our vacation.

5. I have never _____ such a thing.

6. Please _____ on the counter.

G. Listen to the statements and fill in the blanks.

1. Juan _____ bought it _____ for himself.

2. Could you _____ back to me by next month?

3. That was _____ interesting movie.

4. What time do you _____ in the morning?

5. Could I have _____ time?

6. He always _____ such great ideas.

Chant

GO ONLINE for the Chapter 6 Vocabulary and Grammar Chant

ACADEMIC LISTENING

A. What is a family dinner usually like in your country? Write *T* (true) or *F* (false) for each statement.

_____ television/movies   _____ family

_____ travel/trips   _____ friends

_____ outdoor advertisements   _____ the Internet

_____ grocery stores   _____ local markets

B. Discuss your answers in Activity A with a partner.

C. Listen to the talk. Number the parts of the talk in the correct order.

_____ trade on the Silk Road

_____ trade between Europe and the Americas

_____ food in the world's big cities

Listening Strategy

Listening for time markers

Speakers use time markers to explain when something happened. Time markers can provide important details and also help you to understand the order of events. Time markers usually come at the beginning or end of a sentence. Listen to the examples.

In the 1960s, the restaurant opened.

I went there last weekend.

She graduated three years ago.

GO ONLINE
for more
practice

D. Listen to part of the talk. Match the time markers to the statements.

1. In the 15th century, _____

2. By the 1800s, _____

3. Beginning around 1,600 years ago, _____

4. For hundreds of years, _____

a. potatoes from the Americas, for instance, were grown on farms all over Europe.

b. Christopher Columbus discovered new types of plants and animals.

c. spices, salt, and sugar were packed and transported.

d. the Silk Road connected people from Europe and Asia.

E. Listen to the talk again. Circle the correct answers.

1. What did Europeans send back from the Americas?

a. tomatoes and potatoes   b. cows and chickens

2. What was one thing the Silk Road did?

a. connected people from Asia to the Americas   b. connected people in Asia and Europe

3. What does the speaker mean by "a global food system"?

a. people eat many of the same things   b. people get food from all over the world

F. Listen to the talk again. Ask and answer the questions with a partner.

Partner A	Partner B
1. When did Columbus land in the Americas?	2. What was transported from the Americas to Europe?
3. What was transported from Europe to the Americas?	4. What was the Silk Road?
5. What is different about food production today?	6. What is happening to food in the world's big cities?

Discuss the Ideas

G. Work in a small group. Discuss the questions.

1. In your country, what types of food from other countries do people eat?

2. Have people's diets changed in your country in recent years? Why or why not?

3. What do you think about mixing food from two different cultures?

4. Has your diet changed in recent years?

5. Which types of food are the most popular in the world?

6. Which types of food are the most popular where you live?

▲▲▲ SPEAKING

Speaking Task Leading a group discussion

Step 1 PREPARE

GO ONLINE
for more
practice

Pronunciation Skill

Adverb stress
Speakers often stress adjectives and adverbs that describe adjectives. Listen to the examples.

	adverb	adjective
The movie was	**so**	<u>interesting</u>.
The movie was	**really**	<u>exciting</u>.
The movie was	**sort of**	<u>boring</u>.

A. Listen and repeat.

1. really nice
2. very beautiful
3. so funny
4. pretty spicy
5. too difficult
6. sort of cheap

B. Listen and complete the sentences. Then listen again and repeat.

1. He is _____*definitely*_____ good at it.
2. That was _____ cool.
3. The stadium was _____ full.
4. Skydiving is _____ expensive.
5. The movie was _____ long.

C. Listen to two versions of the same sentence. Check the one with greater adverb stress.

1. ☐ first ✓ second
2. ☐ first ☐ second
3. ☐ first ☐ second
4. ☐ first ☐ second
5. ☐ first ☐ second

90 Unit 2 | Chapter 6

D. Listen. Complete the conversations with the words you hear.

1. A: Have you been to the beach yet? It's _____ really _____ beautiful.

    B: Yes, I was there last weekend. I was _____ surprised though. It

    took _____ a long time to get there.

    A: That's true. It's a _____ long drive.

    B: It was worth it. We had a _____ nice time.

2. A: How was the game?

    B: It was _____ good. Our team scored on the final play of the game.

    A: That's _____ great.

    B: It was. It was _____ exciting.

3. A: Did you go to the concert _____ night?

    B: Yes, it was _____ crowded and _____ loud for me.

    The music wasn't _____ good either.

    A: Sorry to hear that. That doesn't sound like _____ fun.

    B: It wasn't fun. My ears are _____ hurting today.

4. A: Have you bought all of your books for this semester?

    B: Yes, they were _____ expensive though.

    A: I know what you mean. I buy all my books used now. They're

    _____ cheaper if you can find used ones.

    B: That's a _____ good idea. I'll have to do that next time.

E. Work with a partner. Practice the conversations in Activity D.

F. Work with a partner. Use the words in the chart to describe where you live.

My house/apartment/dorm	pretty really so somewhat sort of very	far from campus/close to campus expensive/cheap/reasonable quiet/noisy old/new

GO ONLINE
to practice the
conversations

Step 2 SPEAK

A. Fill in the chart. Rank three types of food from other countries that you like most.

Country	Rank

 B. Share your answers in Activity A with a partner.

Speaking Skill

Involving others in a discussion

Good discussions involve everyone in the group. Speakers use many phrases to ask other people what they think and to get everyone involved in the discussion. Listen to the examples.

What's your opinion?

Does anyone have any other ideas to share?

Eduardo, what are your thoughts?

C. Work in a group of three. Practice the conversation. Take turns in the different roles.

A: Let's see. The question says, "What are some ways that international trade has changed people's diets?" What are your thoughts, (Name of Partner B)?

B: Well, I think trade has improved health because people can eat different types of foods from around the world.

A: That's a good point. What do you think, (Name of Partner C)?

C: I have a different opinion. I think it has made people unhealthier. People now buy more salty and sweet snacks. They buy less fresh fruits and vegetables. How about you, (Name of Partner A)?

A: I'm not sure. I have to think about it more.

Word Partners

a popular person

a popular movie

a popular sport

a popular class

a popular restaurant

GO ONLINE
to practice
word partners

Speaking Task

Leading a group discussion

Work in a group of three. Each person leads a discussion for one of the questions in the chart.

Partner A	Partner B	Partner C
What are some challenges to transporting food long distances?	What are some benefits to international trade of food products?	What are some disadvantages to international trade of food products?

Step 3 REPORT

A. Review your conversations. Write notes in the chart.

	Notes
challenges to transporting food	
benefits of international trade of food products	
disadvantages of international trade of food products	

B. Work with a partner from another group. Share your notes in Activity A.

So what do you have for number 1?

Some challenges to transporting food are cost, time, and energy use. How about you?

Step 4 REFLECT

Checklist

Check (✓) the things you learned in Chapter 6.

○ I learned words and phrases for talking about food production.

○ I understood a talk about food traveling globally.

○ I led a discussion by involving others.

Discussion Question

Where do you buy your food from? Why?

Look at the word bank for Unit 2. Check (✓) the words you know. Circle the words you want to learn better.

OXFORD 2000 🔑

Adjectives		Nouns		Verbs	
big	late	cake	knife	bake	leave
bitter	long	city	lemon	become	make
different	main	coffee	meat	buy	mix
expensive	popular	continent	oil	choose	order
fresh	small	cup	oven	cook	pack
frozen	social	event	pan	create	pick
hard	soft	farm	sauce	cut	plant
large	sweet	fish	ship	deliver	prepare
		fork	store	eat	produce
		fruit	vegetable	feed	put
		goods		fry	store
				grow	try
				help	use

PRACTICE WITH THE OXFORD 2000 🔑

A. Use the chart. Match adjectives with nouns.

1. _____bitter coffee_____   2. _____

3. _____   4. _____

5. _____   6. _____

B. Use the chart. Match verbs with nouns.

1. _____buy some vegetables_____   2. _____

3. _____   4. _____

5. _____   6. _____

C. Use the chart. Match verbs with adjective noun partners.

1. _____cook frozen fish_____   2. _____

3. _____   4. _____

5. _____   6. _____

UNIT **3** Science and Technology

CHAPTER **7** | What Is a Green Building?

▲ **VOCABULARY**
- Oxford 2000 🔑 words to talk about the environment

▲▲ **LISTENING**
- Listening for general information
- Listening for cause-effect relationships

▲▲▲ **SPEAKING**
- Practicing minimal pairs
- Describing the environment you live in

CHAPTER **8** | Which Apps Do You Use?

▲ **VOCABULARY**
- Oxford 2000 🔑 words to talk about the Internet

▲▲ **LISTENING**
- Listening to make inferences
- Listening for additional information

▲▲▲ **SPEAKING**
- Practicing intonation for words in a series
- Presenting a web app

CHAPTER **9** | How Do You Get Health Care?

▲ **VOCABULARY**
- Oxford 2000 🔑 words to talk about health care

▲▲ **LISTENING**
- Listening for opinions
- Listening for facts

▲▲▲ **SPEAKING**
- Practicing the schwa /ə/ sound
- Having a group discussion

UNIT WRAP UP | Extend Your Skills

- Use *both*, *either*, and *neither*
- Listen for general information
- Recognize silent letters

- Listen for cause-effect relationships
- Practice minimal pairs
- Describe the environment you live in

▲ VOCABULARY ▶ Oxford 2000 ✎ words to talk about the environment

Learn Words

🔊 **A. Label each picture with the correct word. Then listen and repeat the words and phrases.**

| air-conditioning | fresh | green | heating | natural | paper | power | save |

1.

_____natural_____ light

2.

_____ system

3.

_____ building

4.

_____ unit

5.

wind_____

6.

recycle_____

7.

_____ air

8.

_____ energy

Grammar Note

both, either, and neither

Speakers use conjunctions to join a group of words or phrases. The words *both, either,* and *neither* often join phrases in the following pairs: *both/and, either/or, not only/but also,* and *neither/nor.* Listen to the examples.

> The school has majors in **both** business **and** accounting.
>
> You can eat at **either** the cafeteria **or** the rooftop restaurant.
>
> He is **not only** a math teacher **but also** a science teacher.

The pair *neither/nor* has a negative meaning, so it does not go with other negative words or phrases. Listen to the correct example.

NOT *I don't have **neither** a brother **nor** a sister.*

CORRECT *I have **neither** a brother **nor** a sister.*

B. Complete the statements with the words from the box. Some words will be used more than once. Then listen and check your answers.

both	~~but also~~	either	nor	or

1. Ander has lived not only in many countries in Europe _____but also_____ in many countries in Latin America.

2. I am studying _____ science and engineering at the college.

3. You can take environmental science _____ this semester _____ next semester.

4. I neither like _____ dislike the game. It's just OK.

5. The main dish is served with _____ salad or steamed vegetables.

6. The class runs on _____ weekdays and weekends.

C. Listen and repeat the statements in Activity B.

D. Fix the mistake in each sentence. Then listen and check your answers.

1. You can use the pass for both the subway or the bus.

2. You can take either a cab nor a bus.

3. The room doesn't have neither a window nor an air conditioner.

4. The room has either a heating and a cooling system.

5. She said that we could park in either Lot A and Lot C.

6. We only visited the museum but also went to the shopping district.

Learn Phrases

A. Match each phrase to the correct picture. Then listen and repeat.

collect rainwater	produce harmful gases
control energy use in a building	turn off the lights
have a problem with pollution	take care of the environment
plants improve air quality	use public transportation

1.

2.

3.

4.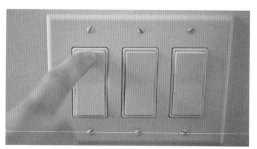

5.

6.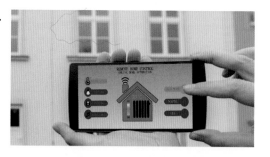

7.

8.

B. Listen to the speakers. Circle the phrase that completes each sentence.

1. The speaker will ⟨*leave for fresh air.*⟩ *go to an office.*

2. The speaker says to *turn off* *turn on* the lights.

3. The speaker suggests *walking.* *taking public transportation.*

4. The speaker wants to take care of the environment by *using less electricity.*
   reducing waste.

5. The speaker says he uses the heating system *rarely.* *often.*

6. The speaker says that collecting rainwater *is expensive.* *is not expensive.*

**C. Check (✓) things that you do to take care of the environment. Then discuss
your answers with a partner.**

☐ I always turn off the lights when I leave a room.	☐ I always turn off electronic equipment after I use it.
☐ I open windows instead of using air-conditioning.	☐ I walk or ride a bike to class instead of driving.
☐ I recycle paper, plastic, and cans.	☐ I wear warm clothing instead of turning on the heating in my home.

**D. Choose one of the buildings from the box. Check (✓) the statements that best
describe the building you chose.**

your childhood home	your high school
the building you are in now	a shopping mall

Building: _____

☐ has air-conditioning	☐ does not have air-conditioning
☐ has plants inside	☐ doesn't have plants inside
☐ close to public transportation	☐ far from public transportation
☐ has a garden	☐ has no garden
☐ has a heating system	☐ does not have a heating system
☐ has lots of natural light	☐ has little or no natural light

**E. Work with a partner. Take turns describing the building you chose in
Activity D.**

GO ONLINE
for more
practice

▲▲ LISTENING

CONVERSATION

🔊 **A. Listen to the conversation. Circle the topics the speakers talk about.**

bus tickets   *garden*   *a green building*   *renting an apartment*

🔊 **B. Listen to the conversation again. Write *T* (true) or *F* (false) for each statement.**

1. _____ The building is close to public transportation.

2. _____ The building gets hot in the summer.

3. _____ The area around the building is expensive.

Listening Strategy

Listening for general information

Listening for general information will help you understand the main ideas and purpose of a conversation. When listening for general information, think about the following:

1. How many speakers are talking?

2. Where are the speakers?

3. What is the main subject of the conversation?

GO ONLINE
for more
practice

🔊 **C. Listen to the first part of the conversation again. Circle the correct answers.**

1. How many speakers are talking?   *one*   *two*   *three*

2. Where are the speakers?   *at an apartment building*   *at an office building*

3. What is purpose of the   *to learn about public*   *to rent an apartment*
   conversation?   *transportation*

🔊 **D. Listen to the second part of the conversation again. Circle the correct answers.**

1. What is the main subject of this part of the conversation?

a. public transportation   b. costs and expenses   c. restaurants in the area

2. Why is the natural cooling system discussed?

a. It helps to save money.   b. It is an interesting part of   c. It costs a little extra money
                                    the building.   to use it.

Recognizing silent letters

🔊 Many words have silent letters that speakers often do not pronounce. Silent letters let speakers say words faster by making them easier to say. Listen to the example.

*I am interested in the program → I'm intre*sted *in the program.*

🔊 **E. Listen and repeat. Then circle the silent letters in the underlined words.**

1. The buildings look quite <u>different</u>.

2. Surinder dropped his new <u>camera</u>.

3. Nori bought some <u>vegetables</u> at the market.

4. The <u>business</u> closed last year.

5. I <u>actually</u> enjoy reading history.

6. Could you buy me a box of <u>chocolate</u>?

🔊 **F. Circle the words with silent letters. Then listen and check your answers.**

1. He works in a laboratory.

2. I'm not sure what the difference is.

3. This couch is so comfortable.

4. He just finished elementary school.

6. We have a really big family.

G. Match the questions and answers.

1. What student groups are you interested in? __b__

2. What is your favorite movie? _____

3. Do you like reading about history? _____

4. What kinds of vegetables do you eat? _____

5. How big is your family? _____

a. I don't have one.

b. ~~The ski club looks good.~~

c. Things like kale, spinach, and bell peppers.

d. There are four people: my mom, my dad, and my two older brothers.

e. Yes, I like the ancient period.

 H. Work with a partner. Ask and answer the questions in Activity H.

Chant

GO ONLINE for the Chapter 7 Vocabulary and Grammar Chant

ACADEMIC LISTENING

A. What are the most important ways for buildings to save energy? Rank the items (most important = 1, least important = 6).

_____ build with recycled materials

_____ collect and use rainwater

_____ control building temperature with a smart system

_____ turn off electronic equipment when it is not used

_____ use natural light for heating

_____ use wind or solar power

B. Work with a partner. Compare your answers in Activity A.

C. Listen to part of the talk. Circle the main subject of the talk.

city recycling programs   *green buildings*   *harmful gases*

D. Listen to part of the talk again. Number the topics in the order they are discussed.

_____ The convention center is a green building.

_____ Buildings use a lot of energy and produce harmful gases.

_____ Green buildings are good for the environment.

E. Listen to the rest of the talk. Check (✓) the items in the talk that describe the convention center.

☐ collects rainwater

☐ has smart doors

☐ has solar power

☐ saves money

☐ uses air-conditioning units

☐ uses natural light

☐ uses recycled paper

☐ uses wind power

Listening for cause-effect relationships

Speakers describe cause-effect relationships to give reasons why something happens. The words/phrases *so*, *because*, *because of*, *since*, and *as a result* signal cause-effect relationships. However, only a noun phrase follows *because of*. Listen to the examples.

cause   **effect**
There was a car accident, so traffic was backed up on the highway.

The subway line added new stops. **As a result**, *more people are using the subway.*

effect   **cause**
He did not pass the exam **because** *he did not study for it.*

I didn't get much sleep **since** *I got in so late last night.*

noun phrase
We were late **because of** *the construction on the road.*

GO ONLINE for more practice

F. Listen to part of the talk again. Match the phrases.

1. natural heating and cooling systems _____
2. makes its own clean power _____
3. many windows for natural light _____

a. the building uses less electricity

b. the building saves a lot of energy

c. the building saves energy and produces fewer harmful gases

G. Listen to part of the talk again. Fill in the cause-effect statements.

1. And _____*because*_____ it collects rainwater, the building uses much less

   _____.

2. The building has balconies and open-air spaces _____ people can

   go outside and get _____.

3. People are really interested in the convention center _____ of its green

   _____.

Discuss the Ideas

H. Work in a small group. Discuss the questions.

1. What interests you about green buildings?

2. What is a good way for buildings to save energy?

3. Are you willing to pay more to live in a green apartment building? Why or why not?

4. Do you think it is important for a city to have good public transportation? Explain.

▲▲▲ SPEAKING

Speaking Task Describing the environment you live in

Step 1 PREPARE

GO ONLINE
for more
practice

Pronunciation Skill

Minimal pairs

◀) Minimal pairs are words that sound similar because they have only one sound that is different between them. Listen to the example.

*The **leaf** is green.*   *I need to **leave** now.*

◀) **A. Listen and repeat the pairs.**

1. work	walk	2. think	thing
3. ship	sheep	4. desk	disk
5. fan	van	6. bad	bed
7. free	three	8. safe	save
9. bay	pay	10. ice	eyes
11. hurt	heart	12. fly	fry

◀) **B. Listen to each statement and circle the word you hear.**

1. I   *worked*   *walked*   for three hours today.

2. I   *think*   *thing*   it's over there.

3. The   *ship*   *sheep*   are on the hill.

4. The   *desk*   *disk*   is in the living room.

5. Could you turn on the   *fan*   *van*?

6. It's on the   *bed.*   *bad.*

7. You can have   *free.*   *three.*

8. You might want to   *safe*   *save*   it.

9. The   *bay*   *pay*   is nice.

10. You can buy   *ice*   *eyes*   across the street.

11. He was   *hurt*   *heart*   during the game.

12. You can   *fly*   *fry*   for free on the airline.

🔊 **C. Listen. Complete the conversations with the words you hear.**

1. A: I like to _____ walk _____ to _____ every day. It takes about 45 minutes.

   B: Wow. That's too long for me. I prefer to drive to _____. It's much faster that way.

   A: That's true, but _____ is much better for the environment and your health, too.

2. A: Is it true that you can take a boat ride around the _____?

   B: Yeah, you can. You _____ $15 for a one-hour trip.

   A: That's not _____. I'm going to do that.

3. A: Has anyone seen the _____ that was on my _____?

   B: No, sorry. Was it in a _____?

   A: No, it wasn't. It was just the _____.

GO ONLINE
to practice the conversations

💬 **D. Work with a partner. Practice the conversations in Activity C.**

E. Match the questions and answers.

1. Do you like to fly? __h__

2. Do you walk to class? _____

3. Do you know how to ice skate? _____

4. Do you have a desk to study at? _____

5. Do you like to sleep with a fan on? _____

6. Do you want to ship the package? _____

7. Do you still work part-time? _____

8. Do you go to bed early on Sundays? _____

9. Do you have to pay to print? _____

10. Do you put plastics in this bin? _____

a. No, I usually ride a bicycle to my classes.

b. Yes, I like my room to be cool when I sleep.

c. No, I actually work full-time now.

d. No, I don't. I have never been on an ice rink.

e. No, that bin is for paper only.

f. Yes, how long will it take?

g. No, I don't. I usually go to the library to study.

h. ~~Not really. I don't like planes.~~

i. Yes, because I have class at 8 AM on Mondays.

j. No, you don't. Printing is free in the lab.

💬 **F. Work with a partner. Ask and answer the questions in Activity E.**

Step 2 SPEAK

 A. Work with a partner. Ask and answer the questions.

1. What is one good point about where you live now?

2. What is one bad point about where you live now?

3. What is one thing that you would like to change about where you live?

Word Partners

take care of a child

take care of a problem

take care of a dog

take care of yourself

take care of business

GO ONLINE
to practice word partners

Speaking Skill

Organizing ideas for speaking

When speakers describe something, they organize their thoughts into parts. This strategy helps improve understanding by making it easier for the listener to follow.

B. Choose one of the topics from the box. Then write down three parts of the topic.

an environmental organization	a green building
the environment in your hometown	green energy

Topic: _____

1. _____

2. _____

3. _____

C. Write notes for each part of the topic you chose in Activity B.

_____

_____

_____

_____

 D. Use your notes in Activities B and C to discuss your topic with a partner.

Speaking Task

Describing the environment you live in

1. Write notes about where you live in the chart.

Inside your home	Around your home	The area/ neighborhood

2. Work with a partner. Take turns describing where you live. Take notes about where your partner lives in the chart.

Inside your partner's home	Around your partner's home	The area/ neighborhood

Step 3 REPORT

Review your notes about your home and your partner's home. Complete the chart with differences and similarities. Then present your findings to the class.

Differences between where you and your partner live	Similarities between where you and your partner live

Step 4 REFLECT

Checklist

Check (✓) the things you learned in Chapter 7.

○ I learned words and phrases for talking about the environment.

○ I understood a talk about green buildings.

○ I had a conversation about where I live.

Discussion Question

What is the most serious environmental problem the world faces? Explain your answer.

CHAPTER 8

Which Apps Do You Use?

- Use *be able to*
- Listen to make inferences
- Recognize pronouns

- Listen for additional information
- Practice intonation for words in a series
- Present a web app

▲ VOCABULARY ▶ Oxford 2000 ⚿ words to talk about the Internet

Learn Words

🔊 **A. Label each picture with the correct word. Then listen and repeat the words and phrases.**

device	email	file	music	search	social	system	video

1.

upload a(n) _____file_____

2.

a mobile _____

3.

a(n) _____ address

4.

a(n) _____ clip

5.

an operating _____

6.

a(n) _____ engine

7.

a(n) _____ networking site

8.

download _____

Grammar Note

be able to

🔊 The phrase *be able to* expresses the ability to do something. Speakers often use *be able to* instead of *can* or *could*. Listen to the examples.

I can use the program.	*I **am able to** use the program.*
I couldn't finish.	*I **wasn't able to** finish dinner.*
Can you come tonight?	***Are** you **able to** come tonight?*

 B. Listen and repeat each statement.

1. Tom is able to join the team.   Tom isn't able to join the team.

2. I'm able to do it.   I'm not able to do it.

3. They'll be able to come.   They won't be able to come.

4. They're going to be able to go.   They aren't going to be able to go.

5. It's able to collect information.   It isn't able to collect information.

6. We're able to take breaks.   We weren't able to take breaks.

C. Circle the answers that are correct for you. Then take turns asking and answering the questions with a partner.

Partner A			Partner B		
1. Are you able to swim?	*Yes, I am.*	*No, I'm not.*	2. Are you able to play a musical instrument?	*Yes, I am.*	*No, I'm not.*
3. Are you able to design a website?	*Yes, I am.*	*No, I'm not.*	4. Are you able meet new people easily?	*Yes, I am.*	*No, I'm not.*
5. Are you able to work well in groups?	*Yes, I am.*	*No, I'm not.*	6. Are you able to speak a foreign language?	*Yes, I am.*	*No, I'm not.*

 D. Work with a partner. Ask and answer the questions.

1. What sports are you able to play?

2. How many languages are you able to speak?

3. What are you going to be able to do with a college degree?

4. What are you able to do now that you weren't able to do when you were young?

Learn Phrases

A. Match each phrase to the correct picture. Then listen and repeat.

check your email	install an app on your phone
comment on a photo	search for products
enter personal information	send it as an attachment

1.

2.

3.

4.

5.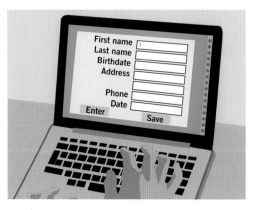

6.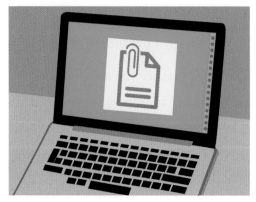

B. Listen to each speaker. Circle the phrase that best represents the main idea.

1. creating an email address online   (providing personal information online)
2. downloading pictures   uploading pictures
3. uploading a software program   installing a software program
4. sending a file through email   an instructor's email to a student
5. commenting on photos   sharing information
6. a web app   a new tablet

C. Check (✓) the phrases you agree with.

Social networking websites…

☐ have improved access to information   ☐ are easy to use

☐ have helped people make friends   ☐ are bad for people's friendships

☐ annoy me   ☐ are fun to use

D. Work with a partner. Discuss your answers in Activity C.

E. Think of a website you use. Check (✓) the statements that describe the website.

Website name: _____

☐ I can upload pictures or videos to the site.

☐ I entered my personal information to make comments on the site.

☐ I installed an app on my phone to use the site.

☐ I can download music from the site.

☐ I search for products that I want to buy on the site.

F. Work in a small group. Describe the website you chose in Activity E in three to four sentences.

GO ONLINE
for more practice

▲▲ LISTENING

CONVERSATION

◀) **A. Listen to the conversation. Circle the topics the speakers discuss.**

search engines   online journals   social networking sites   software companies   web apps

◀) **B. Listen to the conversation again. Circle the correct answers.**

1. Tariq's app   *lets users keep an online journal.*   *tells users about things in an area.*

2. The woman's app   *lets users keep an online journal.*   *tells users about places in an area.*

Listening Strategy

Making inferences

◀) When you make inferences, you make conclusions based on the information that you have heard. Listening for the main idea, a speaker's tone, and thinking about what will happen next can help you make inferences. Listen to the example.

Amber: Are you going to play with us tonight?

Nigel: I don't really play sports, and the last time I played basketball I got hurt.

Inference: Nigel will not play basketball tonight although he does not say so directly.

GO ONLINE
for more
practice

◀) **C. Listen to the speakers. Circle the correct answers.**

1. What is the main idea?   *using a search engine*   *buying things online*

2. What is the speaker's tone about personal information online?   *positive*   *negative*

3. What will happen next?   *The speakers will leave.*   *The speakers will order food.*

◀) **D. Listen to parts of the conversation in Activity A. Circle the correct answers.**

1. What is the woman's tone?   *positive*   *negative*

2. What is the main topic?   *posting content online*   *using a web app*

3. What is Tariq's attitude toward the app?   *He is interested in it.*   *He's not sure about it.*

◀) **E. Listen to the conversation again. Circle the correct inferences.**

1. The woman thinks that Tariq   *uses his phone too much.*   *is good with his phone.*

2. The woman   *might download the online journal app.*   *has tried online journaling.*

3. Tariq will   *likely download*   *not download*   the app the woman describes.

Recognizing pronouns

There are many words in English that sound similar. Possessive pronouns (e.g., *their*) often sound similar to pronouns used with contractions (e.g., *they're*). Listen to the examples.

They're *coming tonight.*   **Their** *house is on this street.*

Who's *she?*   **Whose** *car is this?*

F. Circle the correct form in each sentence.

1. (Whose) Who's   shirt is on the ground?   2. *They're   Their*   meeting us later.

3. *He's   His*   a really nice person.   4. The dog injured   *it's   its*   leg.

5. *You're   Your*   class starts soon.   6. My uncle visited   *are   our*   apartment.

7. *Its   It's*   a useful software program.   8. The plan was   *he's   his*   idea.

G. Listen to each statement and circle the correct form.

1. your   (you're)   2. whose   who's

3. its   it's   4. his   he's

5. their   they're   6. whose   who's

7. his   he's   8. its   it's

H. Complete each question with *who's* or *whose*. Then match the questions and answers.

1. _____Whose_____ smartphone is this? __c__

2. _____ designing our website? _____

3. _____ information was posted? _____

4. _____ going to upload the file? _____

5. _____ tablet is this? _____

6. _____ sending it as an attachment? _____

a. It's his tablet.

b. He's sending it as an attachment.

c. ~~It's my smartphone.~~

d. We're designing it.

e. Her information was posted.

f. Their group is going to upload it.

Chant

GO ONLINE for the Chapter 8 Vocabulary and Grammar Chant

A. Rank your interest (most interested = 6, least interested = 1) in the following types of apps.

_____ chat or video call

_____ design

_____ English language

_____ games

_____ time management

_____ travel

B. Share your answers in Activity A with a partner.

C. Listen to part of the proposal. Circle the correct answers.

1. What is the presenter's goal?   *to sell a web app*   *to find a business partner*

2. What product do the speakers talk about?   *a web app*   *a social networking site*

D. Listen to the whole proposal. Mark _T_ (true) or _F_ (false) for each statement.

1. _____ The app is a medical app.

2. _____ A smartphone camera is used with the app.

3. _____ People can share their designs online.

Listening Strategy

Listening for additional information

Speakers add information when they want to describe something or provide extra details about a topic. Speakers often use signal words and phrases to tell the listener that they are adding information. Listen to the examples.

*The app is very cheap. It's **also** easy to install on your tablet.*

*The tablet is really thin. It has lots of interesting functions, **too**.*

*It has a battery that lasts 40 hours. **Along with** that, it can connect to your computer wirelessly.*

*That store has the best prices. **Another** thing is that it has great customer service.*

*This smartphone has the best camera. **One other point** is that it's easier to use than the other models.*

GO ONLINE
for more
practice

E. Complete the statements with the signal words and phrases from the box. Then listen and check your answers.

along with	also	another good point	one other problem	too

1. Reality apps are becoming popular. They are _____*also*_____ a lot of fun to use.

2. This smartphone comes in several different colors. _____ this option, you can select from three sizes.

3. I use the site to get price information on new products. It has reviews of products, _____.

4. It's really expensive. _____ is that it doesn't work very well.

5. Electronic books are cheaper. _____ is that they're easier to take notes with.

F. Listen to statements from the proposal. Circle the signal words and phrases you hear.

1. also   (along with)   too

2. also   one other thing   another thing

3. also   along with   too

4. also   along with   too

G. Listen to the whole proposal again. Ask and answer the questions with a partner.

Partner A	Partner B
1. What kind of app is discussed?	2. How much money does the presenter want?
3. What is the purpose of the web app?	4. What kinds of things does the app search for?
5. How do users know how products look in a room?	6. Why does the speaker not find an investor?

Discuss the Ideas

H. Work in a small group. Discuss the questions.

1. Do you think smartphones have improved people's lives? Why or why not?

2. How many web apps do you use?

3. Why do you think web apps are so popular?

4. What do you think about the web apps discussed in the two listening sections? Which one did you like most?

5. What do you think about reality apps?

▲▲▲ SPEAKING

Speaking Task Presenting a web app

Step 1 PREPARE

Pronunciation Skill

Intonation for words in a series

🔊 Intonation is the rising and falling of a person's voice. For words in a series, a speaker's voice rises and then falls for the last word in a series. Listen to the example.

rising   rising   falling

↘   ↘   ↗

They went to the mall, the grocery store, and the bank.

GO ONLINE
for more
practice

🔊 **A. Listen and repeat the statements.**

1. The app allows users to download music, upload images, and create new content.

2. Web apps are cheap, convenient, and user-friendly.

3. When you install the app, type in your name, password, and email address.

4. You can take the bus, subway, or train.

5. I tried Thai, Greek, and Colombian food at the international festival.

6. The building uses a combination of wind, solar, and electric power.

7. Tom studied math, English, and visual art.

🔊 **B. Listen. Complete the conversation with the words you hear.**

A: Hey, I found this new social networking site for people who want to do a

_____ exchange.

B: I don't know. I use too many social networking sites already.

A: Yeah, but this site is different. You meet new _____, learn about

_____, and study a _____.

B: It sounds interesting, but I want to spend my free time doing something else. I'm

already taking English classes in grammar, writing, and _____

this semester.

🔊 **C. Listen to the conversation in Activity B again. Draw arrows to mark rising (↘) and falling intonation (↗).**

D. Listen. Complete the conversation with the words you hear.

A: OK, everyone. As you know, you need to register for the class _____.
To do so, you need to enter your _____, _____, and
student ID number.

B: Sorry, I have a question. I didn't get my student ID _____ yet. Can I
still register for the class website?

A: Yes, you can. I just need you to send me an email with your full name,
birthdate, and email _____. Then I'll send you a
password that will let you register for the class website.

B: Thank you. I'll do that.

A: The class website is a really important _____ of the class. We'll use it
for class discussions, assignments, and _____. So be sure that you
register right away.

B: Can you tell me if the class discussions are graded?

A: Good question. No, they are not graded, but everyone should try to participate in the
discussions.

B: How do we participate?

A: There are several ways to get involved. You can ask _____, make
comments, and _____ information.

GO ONLINE to practice the conversation

E. Work with a partner. Practice the conversation in Activity D.

F. Complete each sentence with a series of words or phrases.

1. This classroom has _____, _____, and
_____.

2. There is _____, _____, and _____
in my bedroom.

3. I would like to visit _____, _____, and
_____ someday.

4. I like to _____, _____, and _____
in my free time.

G. Share your answers in Activity F with a partner.

Step 2 SPEAK

 A. Work in a small group. Complete the chart.

	Name of site	Reason
a good website for buying clothing		
a good website for downloading web apps		
a good website for social networking		

Word Partners

a smart person

a smart plan

a smart idea

a smart home

look smart

GO ONLINE
to practice
word partners

Speaking Skill

Giving short presentations

Organizing your ideas is important when giving a short presentation. It is helpful to use notes when you give a presentation. However, you should not read every word of your presentation from notes.

Presentation	Useful phrases	Notes
1. Topic	I am presenting on XYZ.com. My presentation is on XYZ. com.	
2. Important point	The site lets you... The site has...	
Example/ additional information	For example, the website lets users... It also...	
3. Important point	It can help you to...	
Example/ additional information	So you can... You can also use it to...	
4. Conclusion	It is really useful. The website helps me save a lot of time. It is a great site for...	

 B. Work with a partner. Think of a website you use. Complete the chart in the Speaking Skill box.

C. Work in a group. Give a presentation of four to five sentences on your website.

Speaking Task

Presenting a web app

1. Work in a small group. Answer the questions.
   - What is a web app that you like?
   - What do you like about it?
   - Where can you download it?
   - What are you able to do with it?

2. Organize your notes for a presentation on a web app that you like.

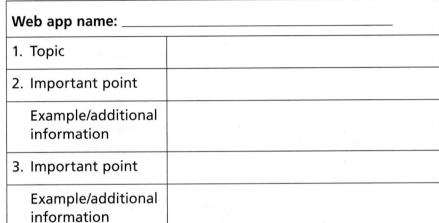

Web app name: _____

1. Topic	
2. Important point	
Example/additional information	
3. Important point	
Example/additional information	
4. Conclusion	

3. Present your web app to a partner. What did you like about your partner's presentation? What else do you want to know about your partner's web app?

Step 3 REPORT

Think about the presentations you heard. Answer the questions.

1. Which app do you think is the most useful? Why is it useful?

2. Do you want to download any of the apps you heard about?

Step 4 REFLECT

Checklist

Check (✓) the things you learned in Chapter 8.

○ I learned words and phrases for talking about the Internet.

○ I understood a talk about web apps.

○ I gave a short presentation on a web app.

Discussion Question

How has the Internet changed people's lives?

CHAPTER 9

How Do You Get Health Care?

- Use *used to*
- Listen for opinions
- Recognize meaning in intonation

- Listen for facts
- Practice the schwa /ə/ sound
- Have a group discussion

▲ VOCABULARY ▶ Oxford 2000 🔑 words to talk about health care

Learn Words

🔊 **A. Label each picture with the correct word. Then listen and repeat the words and phrases.**

| card | clinic | doctor | medicine | patient | pharmacy | sick | throat |

1.

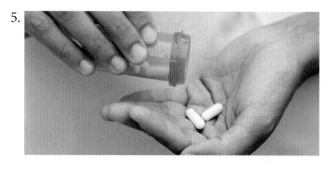

a sore _____throat_____

2.

a hospital _____

3.

get _____

4.

a health _____

5.

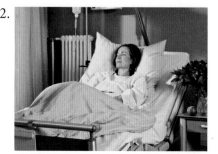

take _____

6.

a local _____

7.

go to see a _____

8.

a health _____

Grammar Note

used to

🔊 The phrase *used to* describes something that happened frequently in the past but does not happen anymore. Listen to the example.

> I **used to** work on a farm every summer.

When used in the negative, *used to* becomes *use to*. Listen to the example.

> I didn't **use to** play video games that much.

For an action completed at a point in time without frequency, do not use *used to*. Listen to the example.

> I played basketball last week.

In questions, *used to* becomes *use to*. Listen to the example.

> What did you **use to** study in college?

🔊 **B. Listen and repeat each statement.**

1. He used to work at the bank.

2. I used to live there.

3. It used to be so much fun.

4. They didn't use to work such long hours.

C. Check (✓) the statements that use *used to* correctly.

1. ☐ I used to go there last night.

2. ☐ They used to go bowling once a week.

3. ☐ She used to work there.

4. ☐ We used to visit every summer.

5. ☐ We used to live abroad years ago.

6. ☐ He didn't used to like it.

D. Match the questions and answers.

1. What did you use to do for fun as a child? __c__

2. What did you use to do in high school? _____

3. What did you use to do with your family when you were young? _____

a. I used to wear a uniform to school when I was in high school.

b. My family and I used to go on vacation together every summer.

c. ~~I used to ride my bicycle a lot as a child.~~

E. Complete the statements. Then share your answers with a partner.

1. When I was a young child, I used to _____.

2. When I was in high school, I used to _____.

3. My family and I used to _____.

Learn Phrases

A. Match each phrase to the correct picture. Then listen and repeat.

buy medicine at the pharmacy	have a serious illness
get a prescription	make an appointment to see a doctor
have a bad cough	stay in bed
have a high temperature	take care of someone

1.
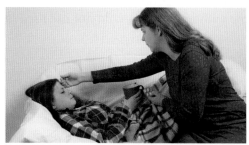

_____

2.

_____

3.

_____

4.

_____

5.

_____

6.

_____

7.

_____

8.
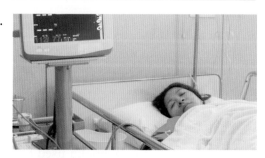

_____

B. Listen to each speaker. Mark _T_ (true) or _F_ (false) for each statement.

1. __F__ The local health clinic takes student health cards.

2. _____ There is a pharmacy on campus.

3. _____ The man gets a health checkup every year.

4. _____ The nurse helped the woman while she was in the hospital.

5. _____ The man got a prescription from the doctor.

6. _____ The woman got medicine from the doctor.

C. Match the questions and responses.

1. How do I get a prescription? __e__

2. Where is the health clinic? _____

3. What should I take for a sore throat? _____

4. How long have you had a cough? _____

5. How often do you get sick? _____

a. I don't get sick very often. Maybe once a year.

b. Just drink some hot tea and a lot of water.

c. It's in the Student Services building.

d. I have had it for about a week.

e. ~~You need to see a doctor.~~

D. Ask and answer the questions in Activity C with a partner.

E. Check (✓) the items that are true for you.

1. I have…

☐ a student health card   ☐ a national health card   ☐ traveler's health insurance

2. I usually get medicine at…

☐ a pharmacy   ☐ a store   ☐ a health clinic

3. I get…

☐ a health checkup every year   ☐ a monthly health checkup

4. When I get sick, I…

☐ visit a doctor   ☐ stay in bed and get rest

5. This year I have had … at least once.

☐ a bad cough   ☐ a store   ☐ a high fever

GO ONLINE
for more
practice

▲▲ LISTENING

CONVERSATION

🔊 **A. Listen to the conversation. Circle the topics the speakers discuss.**

a student health program   *studying medicine*

the campus pharmacy   *a student health center*

🔊 **B. Listen to the conversation again. Circle the correct answers.**

1. The woman   *likes*   *dislikes*   the health program.

2. The man likes the health program because   *it is cheap.*   *it is convenient.*

3. The woman says she gets medicine from   *a hospital*   *a local pharmacy*   if she needs it.

Listening Strategy

Listening for opinions

🔊 Speakers often use phrases to signal that they are giving their opinion. Listen to the examples:

> **In my view**, *the book was a little boring.*

> **I think** *it's a great idea.*

> **My personal feeling** *is that we should wait.*

GO ONLINE
for more
practice

💬 **C. Complete each statement with your opinion. Then share your answers with a partner.**

1. In my opinion, health services for students at my school are _____.

2. If you ask me, _____ is the best thing to do when you get sick.

3. I believe that _____ is a good way to stay healthy.

4. I think _____ is a good thing to drink when you have a sore throat.

💬 **D. Work with a partner. Discuss the questions.**

1. Which person do you agree with in the conversation in Activity A? Explain your answer.

2. Does your school have a student health program?

3. Do you buy traveler's health insurance when you go abroad? Why or why not?

Meaning in intonation

🔊 Intonation is how high or low a person's voice is. The same sentences can have a different meaning depending on a speaker's intonation. Listen to the examples.

 *I didn't know there was an exam tomorrow.*

surprise   **fear**

 *The doctor said I was OK.*

disappointment   **happiness**

 *I have to take the train tomorrow.*

anger   **excitement**

🔊 **E. Listen and repeat each statement. Match the intonation you hear.**

1. It took me about an hour to get downtown.
2. I never get sick enough to use a health center.
3. The professor said the test is next week.
4. The health plan costs $200 a semester.
5. The cafeteria is serving fried rice again.
6. That class is different.

🔊 **F. Listen to the speaker's intonation and circle the meaning of the sentence.**

1. You used to work there?   (surprise)   *anger*   *disappointment*
2. The health clinic is OK.   *surprise*   *excitement*   *disappointment*
3. He is coming.   *happiness*   *anger*   *fear*
4. The lecture was about two hours.   *excitement*   *anger*   *disappointment*

Chant

GO ONLINE for the Chapter 9 Vocabulary and Grammar Chant

ACADEMIC LISTENING

A. Match the different ways of paying for health care.

1. _____ out of pocket

2. _____ national health insurance

3. _____ private insurance

a. pay an insurance company to get health services

b. pay cash only when health services are used

c. pay taxes into a government health program

B. Work with a partner. Which system in Activity A do you know the most about? Explain your answer.

C. Listen to the talk. Circle the correct answers.

1. What is the main topic of the talk?

a. health care systems   b. traveling doctors

2. How does the speaker describe different health care systems?

a. gives good points   b. gives both good and bad points

D. Listen to the talk again. Mark _T_ (true) or _F_ (false) for each statement.

1. _____ The speaker talks about two different health care systems.

2. _____ The speaker talks about an out-of-pocket system.

3. _____ The speaker talks about a national health care system.

4. _____ The speaker gives her opinion on the best health care system.

5. _____ The speaker wants to change her country's health care system.

Listening Strategy

Listening for facts

Speakers often use facts to support what they are saying or to explain something in more detail. Opinions are feelings that people have, but facts are true statements. Listen to the examples.

fact	**fact**
The capital of Uzbekistan is Tashkent.	_The subway costs $2 per ride._
opinion	**opinion**
Tashkent is beautiful.	_The subway is inexpensive._

GO ONLINE
for more
practice

E. Mark if each statement is a fact (*F*) or an opinion (*O*).

1. __*O*__ The new program is a waste of money.

2. _____ Five hundred people use the program each year.

3. _____ Lake Baikal in Russia is the deepest lake in the world.

4. _____ The health system is expensive.

5. _____ There are good points and bad points.

6. _____ People pay taxes into the system.

7. _____ He pays 40 percent of his health care expenses.

8. _____ The health clinic provides high-quality care.

F. Listen to part of the talk again. Check (✓) the facts you hear.

1. [✓] Taxes are paid into a public health care system.

2. [ ] Most people use health clinics in public health care systems.

3. [ ] In Canada, 70 percent of patient's fees are paid by the public health care system.

4. [ ] Private insurance is the most expensive system.

5. [ ] An insurance company pays a doctor for health services in the private system.

6. [ ] People spend $8,500 a year on health care expenses.

7. [ ] Most countries use a mix of health care systems.

G. Listen to the talk again. Ask and answer the questions with a partner.

Partner A	Partner B
1. What is the talk about? 3. How does a public health care system work? 5. What is one bad point given in the talk?	2. What is an out-of-pocket system? 4. How does a private health care system work? 6. What does the speaker think about different health care systems?

Discuss the Ideas

H. Work in a small group. Discuss the questions.

1. Do you know about other health care systems not described in the talk? Explain your answer.

2. Where can you go for health services if you need them?

3. What is a challenge for international students when using health care?

SPEAKING

Speaking Task Having a group discussion

Step 1 PREPARE

Pronunciation Skill

The schwa /ə/ sound

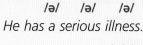 The schwa (/ə/) sound is the most common vowel sound in English. Schwa is a short u sound that allows speakers to say unstressed sounds quickly. Listen to the examples.

/ə/   /ə/   /ə/
He has a serious illness.

/ə/ /ə/
She just finished the examination.

GO ONLINE
for more
practice

A. Listen and repeat.

1. banana	The banana looks old.
2. occur	The sound occurs every hour.
3. about	It's about $10.
4. present	She gave me a present for my birthday.
5. recommend	They recommended this hotel.
6. medicine	The doctor gave me a prescription for the medicine.
7. assist	The nurse assisted the doctor.
8. separate	They live in separate buildings.

B. Circle the words that you think have a schwa sound. Then listen and check your answers.

1. It's a very good system.

2. She arrived around 8 AM.

3. You have to focus on your examination.

4. What color is it?

5. The movie was excellent.

6. My brother lives in California.

7. The team finished the report on time.

8. I saw an elephant at the zoo.

C. Listen. Complete each conversation with the words from the box.

1.

company	different	~~government~~	private	system

A: In my country, the _____government_____ provides health care to everyone by collecting taxes.

B: That's interesting. Where I am from the _____ is quite

_____.

A: How so?

B: Workers don't pay taxes for health care. They pay a _____ health

insurance _____.

2.

appointment	facility	medicine	pharmacy	terrible

A: I have a _____ cough.

B: Sorry to hear that. I had a bad cough last week, so I went to the _____

and got some cough _____. I am feeling much better.

A: I was actually thinking of going to the health clinic on campus.

B: You could do that, too. It's in a brand-new _____. I'm sure they will

take good care of you.

A: That's good. Do you know if I have to make an _____ to see a

doctor?

B: No, I don't think so. You can just walk in and wait to be seen.

3.

horrible	problem	serious	symptoms	trouble	visit

A: Hello, I'm Doctor Bullough. What seems to be the _____?

B: I feel _____, and I have a really _____ cough.

A: I see. Are you having _____ breathing?

B: A little.

A: I see. What other _____ do you have?

B: I guess I have a sore throat.

A: OK, I'm going to write you a prescription, and I want you to come back for another

_____ in two days.

GO ONLINE
to practice the
conversations

 D. Work with a partner. Practice the conversations in Activity C.

Step 2 SPEAK

 A. Work with a partner. Discuss the questions.

1. Should health care be free for college students?

2. What is the best way to improve health and medical services?

Word Partners

take a pill

take your time

take a walk

take a nap

take a look

take a bus

take home

GO ONLINE
to practice
word partners

Speaking Skill

Agreeing and disagreeing

When speakers give their opinions on a topic, they may agree or disagree. The phrases below describe ways to agree and disagree with an opinion. Listen to the examples.

	Agreement	Disagreement
strong	I totally agree with you.	I completely disagree with that idea.
moderate	I agree with you. That's the same way I feel.	I don't think that is correct. I feel differently.
softer	That seems right to me.	I'm not so sure.

B. Listen. Complete each discussion with a phrase from the Speaking Skill box.

1. Topic: What makes a good doctor?

A: What do you think makes a good doctor?

B: I think a good doctor is very highly skilled and knows medicine very well. What about you?

A: Well, _____. Skills are important, but I think a good doctor cares about her patients.

2. Topic: What is the best medicine when you have a cold?

A: What's your opinion?

B: In my view, the best medicine is sleep and healthy eating.

A: _____. Every time I am sick, I stay home and relax.

C. Respond to the topic statement. Write notes in the chart.

Topic	Agree/disagree	Reason
The government should provide free health care.		

 D. Discuss your notes in Activity C with a partner.

Speaking Task

Having a group discussion

1. Respond to each statement. Write notes in the chart.

Health and medicine topics	Agree/ disagree	Reason
Using new technology is the best way to improve health care.		
The biggest problem with health care is that there are not enough doctors.		

2. Work in a small group. Discuss what you wrote in the chart.

Step 3 REPORT

Think about your group discussion.

1. Add notes to your chart in the Speaking Task.

2. Choose one of the topics from the Speaking Task. Write three to five sentences on your opinion.

Step 4 REFLECT

Checklist

Check (✓) the things you learned in Chapter 9.

○ I learned words and phrases for talking about health care.

○ I understood a talk about health care.

○ I had a conversation about health care.

Discussion Question

What do you think is the biggest challenge in health care today?

Extend Your Skills

Look at the word bank for Unit 3. Check (✓) the words you know. Circle the words you want to learn better.

OXFORD 2000 🔑				Verbs	
Adjectives	**Nouns**				
bad	building	information	product	check	produce
fresh	card	light	quality	collect	save
harmful	company	medicine	rain	comment	search
natural	doctor	music	system	control	send
private	email	paper	throat	cough	stay
public	energy	patient	transportation	design	switch
serious	environment	phone	trouble	enter	take
sick	file	photo	video	get	use
social	gas	pollution	water	improve	visit
terrible	government	power	wind	make	
thin	illness				

PRACTICE WITH THE OXFORD 2000 🔑

A. Use the chart. Match adjectives with nouns.

1. _____harmful products_____   2. _____

3. _____   4. _____

5. _____   6. _____

B. Use the chart. Match verbs with nouns.

1. _____produce pollution_____   2. _____

3. _____   4. _____

5. _____   6. _____

C. Use the chart. Match verbs with adjective noun partners.

1. _____make natural power_____   2. _____

3. _____   4. _____

5. _____   6. _____

THE OXFORD 2000 ⚷ LIST OF KEYWORDS

This is a list of the 2000 most important and useful words to learn at this stage in your language learning. These words have been carefully chosen by a group of language experts and experienced teachers, who have judged the words to be important and useful for three reasons.

- Words that are used very **frequently** (= very often) in English are included in this list. Frequency information has been gathered from the American English section of the Oxford English Corpus, which is a collection of written and spoken texts containing over 2 billion words.

- The keywords are frequent across a **range** of different types of text. This means that the keywords are often used in a variety of contexts, not just in newspapers or in scientific articles for example.

- The list includes some important words which are very **familiar** to most users of English, even though they are not used very frequently. These include, for example, words which are useful for explaining what you mean when you do not know the exact word for something.

Names of people, places, etc. beginning with a capital letter are not included in the list of 2000 keywords. Keywords which are not included in the list are numbers, days of the week, and the months of the year.

A

a, an *indefinite article*
ability *n.*
able *adj.*
about *adv., prep.*
above *prep., adv.*
absolutely *adv.*
academic *adj.*
accept *v.*
acceptable *adj.*
accident *n.*
    by accident
according to prep.
account *n.*
accurate *adj.*
accuse *v.*
achieve *v.*
achievement *n.*
acid *n.*
across *adv., prep.*
act *n., v.*
action *n.*
active *adj.*
activity *n.*
actor, actress *n.*
actual *adj.*
actually *adv.*
add *v.*
address *n.*
admire *v.*
admit *v.*
adult *n.*
advanced *adj.*
advantage *n.*
adventure *n.*
advertisement *n.*
advice *n.*

advise *v.*
affect *v.*
afford *v.*
afraid *adj.*
after *prep., conj., adv.*
afternoon *n.*
afterward *adv.*
again *adv.*
against *prep.*
age *n.*
    aged *adj.*
ago *adv.*
agree *v.*
agreement *n.*
ahead *adv.*
aim *n., v.*
air *n.*
airplane *n.*
airport *n.*
alarm *n.*
alcohol *n.*
alcoholic *adj.*
alive *adj.*
all *adj., pron., adv.*
allow *v.*
all right *adj., adv.,*
    exclamation
almost *adv.*
alone *adj., adv.*
along *prep., adv.*
alphabet *n.*
already *adv.*
also *adv.*
although *conj.*
always *adv.*
among *prep.*
amount *n.*

amuse *v.*
analyze *v.*
analysis *n.*
ancient *adj.*
and *conj.*
anger *n.*
angle *n.*
angry *adj.*
animal *n.*
announce *v.*
another *adj., pron.*
answer *n., v.*
any *adj., pron., adv.*
anymore *(also* any more)
    adv.
anyone *(also* anybody)
    pron.
anything *pron.*
anyway *adv.*
anywhere *adv.*
apart *adv.*
apartment *n.*
apparently *adv.*
appear *v.*
appearance *n.*
apple *n.*
apply *v.*
appointment *n.*
appreciate *v.*
appropriate *adj.*
approve *v.*
area *n.*
argue *v.*
argument *n.*
arm *n.*
army *n.*
around *adv., prep.*

arrange *v.*
arrangement *n.*
arrest *v.*
arrive *v.*
arrow *n.*
art *n.*
article *n.*
artificial *adj.*
artist *n.*
artistic *adj.*
as *prep., conj.*
ashamed *adj.*
ask *v.*
asleep *adj.*
at *prep.*
atmosphere *n.*
atom *n.*
attach *v.*
attack *n., v.*
attention *n.*
attitude *n.*
attract *v.*
attractive *adj.*
aunt *n.*
authority *n.*
available *adj.*
average *adj., n.*
avoid *v.*
awake *adj.*
aware *adj.*
away *adv.*

B

baby *n.*
back *n., adj., adv.*
backward *adv.*
bad *adj.*

badly *adv.*
bag *n.*
bake *v.*
balance *n.*
ball *n.*
band *n.*
bank *n.*
bar *n.*
base *n., v.*
baseball *n.*
basic *adj.*
basis *n.*
bath *n.*
bathroom *n.*
be *v.*
beach *n.*
bear *v.*
beard *n.*
beat *v.*
beautiful *adj.*
beauty *n.*
because *conj.*
become *v.*
bed *n.*
bedroom *n.*
beer *n.*
before *prep., conj., adv.*
begin *v.*
beginning *n.*
behave *v.*
behavior *n.*
behind *prep., adv.*
belief *n.*
believe *v.*
bell *n.*
belong *v.*
below *prep., adv.*
belt *n.*
bend *v.*
benefit *n.*
beside *prep.*
best *adj., adv., n.*
better *adj., adv.*
between *prep., adv.*
beyond *prep., adv.*
bicycle *n.*
big *adj.*
bill *n.*
bird *n.*
birth *n.*
birthday *n.*
bite *v.*
bitter *adj.*
black *adj.*
blame *v.*
block *n.*
blood *n.*
blow *v., n.*
blue *adj., n.*

board *n.*
boat *n.*
body *n.*
boil *v.*
bomb *n., v.*
bone *n.*
book *n.*
boot *n.*
border *n.*
bored *adj.*
boring *adj.*
born: be born *v.*
borrow *v.*
boss *n.*
both *adj., pron.*
bother *v.*
bottle *n.*
bottom *n.*
bowl *n.*
box *n.*
boy *n.*
boyfriend *n.*
brain *n.*
branch *n.*
brave *adj.*
bread *n.*
break *v.*
breakfast *n.*
breath *n.*
breathe *v.*
brick *n.*
bridge *n.*
brief *adj.*
bright *adj.*
bring *v.*
broken *adj.*
brother *n.*
brown *adj., n.*
brush *n., v.*
bubble *n.*
build *v.*
building *n.*
bullet *n.*
burn *v.*
burst *v.*
bury *v.*
bus *n.*
bush *n.*
business *n.*
busy *adj.*
but *conj.*
butter *n.*
button *n.*
buy *v.*
by *prep.*
bye *exclamation*

C

cabinet *n.*

cake *n.*
calculate *v.*
call *v., n.*
calm *adj.*
camera *n.*
camp *n., v.*
can *modal v., n.*
cancel *v.*
candy *n.*
capable *adj.*
capital *n.*
car *n.*
card *n.*
care *n., v.*
   take care of
   care for
career *n.*
careful *adj.*
carefully *adv.*
careless *adj.*
carelessly *adv.*
carry *v.*
case *n.*
   in case (of)
cash *n.*
cat *n.*
catch *v.*
cause *n., v.*
CD *n.*
ceiling *n.*
celebrate *v.*
cell *n.*
cell phone *n.*
cent *n.*
center *n.*
centimeter *n.*
central *adj.*
century *n.*
ceremony *n.*
certain *adj.*
certainly *adv.*
chain *n., v.*
chair *n.*
challenge *n.*
chance *n.*
change *v., n.*
character *n.*
characteristic *n.*
charge *n., v.*
charity *n.*
chase *v., n.*
cheap *adj.*
cheat *v.*
check *v., n.*
cheek *n.*
cheese *n.*
chemical *adj., n.*
chemistry *n.*
chest *n.*

chicken *n.*
chief *adj., n.*
child *n.*
childhood *n.*
chin *n.*
chocolate *n.*
choice *n.*
choose *v.*
church *n.*
cigarette *n.*
circle *n.*
citizen *n.*
city *n.*
class *n.*
clean *adj., v.*
clear *adj., v.*
clearly *adv.*
climate *n.*
climb *v.*
clock *n.*
close /kloʊs/ *adj., adv.*
close /kloʊz/ *v.*
closed *adj.*
cloth *n.*
clothes *n.*
clothing *n.*
cloud *n.*
club *n.*
coast *n.*
coat *n.*
coffee *n.*
coin *n.*
cold *adj., n.*
collect *v.*
collection *n.*
college *n.*
color *n., v.*
column *n.*
combination *n.*
combine *v.*
come *v.*
comfortable *adj.*
command *n.*
comment *n., v.*
common *adj.*
communicate *v.*
communication *n.*
community *n.*
company *n.*
compare *v.*
comparison *n.*
competition *n.*
complain *v.*
complaint *n.*
complete *adj.*
completely *adv.*
complicated *adj.*
computer *n.*
concentrate *v.*

concert *n.*
conclusion *n.*
condition *n.*
confidence *n.*
confident *adj.*
confuse *v.*
confused *adj.*
connect *v.*
connection *n.*
conscious *adj.*
consider *v.*
consist *v.*
constant *adj.*
contact *n., v.*
contain *v.*
container *n.*
continent *n.*
continue *v.*
continuous *adj.*
contract *n.*
contrast *n.*
contribute *v.*
control *n., v.*
convenient *adj.*
conversation *n.*
convince *v.*
cook *v.*
cookie *n.*
cooking *n.*
cool *adj.*
copy *n., v.*
corner *n.*
correct *adj., v.*
correctly *adv.*
cost *n., v.*
cotton *n.*
cough *v.*
could *modal v.*
count *v.*
country *n.*
county *n.*
couple *n.*
course *n.*
   of course
court *n.*
cousin *n.*
cover *v., n.*
covering *n.*
cow *n.*
crack *v.*
crash *n., v.*
crazy *adj.*
cream *n., adj.*
create *v.*
credit card *n.*
crime *n.*
criminal *adj., n.*
crisis *n.*
criticism *n.*

criticize *v.*
cross *v.*
crowd *n.*
cruel *adj.*
crush *v.*
cry *v.*
culture *n.*
cup *n.*
curly *adj.*
curve *n.*
curved *adj.*
custom *n.*
customer *n.*
cut *v., n.*

D
dad *n.*
damage *n., v.*
dance *n., v.*
dancer *n.*
danger *n.*
dangerous *adj.*
dark *adj., n.*
date *n.*
daughter *n.*
day *n.*
dead *adj.*
deal *v.*
dear *adj.*
death *n.*
debt *n.*
decide *v.*
decision *n.*
decorate *v.*
deep *adj.*
deeply *adv.*
defeat *v.*
definite *adj.*
definitely *adv.*
definition *n.*
degree *n.*
deliberately *adv.*
deliver *v.*
demand *n., v.*
dentist *n.*
deny *v.*
department *n.*
depend *v.*
depression *n.*
describe *v.*
description *n.*
desert *n.*
deserve *v.*
design *n., v.*
desk *n.*
despite *prep.*
destroy *v.*
detail *n.*
   in detail

determination *n.*
determined *adj.*
develop *v.*
development *n.*
device *n.*
diagram *n.*
dictionary *n.*
die *v.*
difference *n.*
different *adj.*
difficult *adj.*
difficulty *n.*
dig *v.*
dinner *n.*
direct *adj., adv., v.*
direction *n.*
directly *adv.*
dirt *n.*
dirty *adj.*
disadvantage *n.*
disagree *v.*
disagreement *n.*
disappear *v.*
disappoint *v.*
disaster *n.*
discover *v.*
discuss *v.*
discussion *n.*
disease *n.*
disgusting *adj.*
dish *n.*
dishonest *adj.*
disk *n.*
distance *n.*
distant *adj.*
disturb *v.*
divide *v.*
division *n.*
divorce *n., v.*
do *v., auxiliary v.*
doctor *n. (abbr.* Dr.)
document *n.*
dog *n.*
dollar *n.*
door *n.*
dot *n.*
double *adj.*
doubt *n.*
down *adv., prep.*
downstairs *adv., adj.*
downward *adv.*
draw *v.*
drawer *n.*
drawing *n*
dream *n., v.*
dress *n., v.*
drink *n., v.*
drive *v., n.*
driver *n.*

drop *v., n.*
drug *n.*
dry *adj., v.*
during *prep.*
dust *n.*
duty *n.*
DVD *n.*

E
each *adj., pron.*
each other *pron.*
ear *n.*
early *adj., adv.*
earn *v.*
earth *n.*
easily *adv.*
east *n., adj., adv.*
eastern *adj.*
easy *adj.*
eat *v.*
economic *adj.*
economy *n.*
edge *n.*
educate *v.*
education *n.*
effect *n.*
effort *n.*
e.g. *abbr.*
egg *n.*
either *adj., pron., adv.*
election *n.*
electric *adj.*
electrical *adj.*
electricity *n.*
electronic *adj.*
else *adv.*
e-mail *(also* email) *n., v.*
embarrass *v.*
embarrassed *adj.*
emergency *n.*
emotion *n.*
employ *v.*
employment *n.*
empty *adj.*
encourage *v.*
end *n., v.*
   in the end
enemy *n.*
energy *n.*
engine *n.*
enjoy *v.*
enjoyable *adj.*
enjoyment *n.*
enough *adj., pron., adv.*
enter *v.*
entertain *v.*
entertainment *n.*
enthusiasm *n.*
enthusiastic *adj.*

The Oxford 2000 List of Keywords

entrance *n.*
environment *n.*
equal *adj.*
equipment *n.*
error *n.*
escape *v.*
especially *adv.*
essential *adj.*
etc. *abbr.*
even *adv.*
evening *n.*
event *n.*
ever *adv.*
every *adj.*
everybody *pron.*
everyone *pron.*
everything *pron.*
everywhere *adv.*
evidence *n.*
evil *adj.*
exact *adj.*
exactly *adv.*
exaggerate *v.*
exam *n.*
examination *n.*
examine *v.*
example *n.*
excellent *adj.*
except *prep.*
exchange *v., n.*
excited *adj.*
excitement *n.*
exciting *adj.*
excuse *n., v.*
exercise *n.*
exist *v.*
exit *n.*
expect *v.*
expensive *adj.*
experience *n., v.*
experiment *n.*
expert *n.*
explain *v.*
explanation *n.*
explode *v.*
explore *v.*
explosion *n.*
expression *n.*
extra *adj., adv.*
extreme *adj.*
extremely *adv.*
eye *n.*

F

face *n., v.*
fact *n.*
factory *n.*
fail *v.*
failure *n.*

fair *adj.*
fall *v., n.*
false *adj.*
familiar *adj.*
family *n.*
famous *adj.*
far *adv., adj.*
farm *n.*
farmer *n.*
fashion *n.*
fashionable *adj.*
fast *adj., adv.*
fasten *v.*
fat *adj., n.*
father *n.*
fault *n.*
favor *n.*
   in favor
favorite *adj., n.*
fear *n., v.*
feather *n.*
feature *n.*
feed *v.*
feel *v.*
feeling *n.*
female *adj.*
fence *n.*
festival *n.*
few *adj., pron.*
   a few
field *n.*
fight *v., n.*
figure *n.*
file *n.*
fill *v.*
film *n.*
final *adj.*
finally *adv.*
financial *adj.*
find *v.*
   find out sth
fine *adj.*
finger *n.*
finish *v.*
fire *n., v.*
firm *n., adj.*
firmly *adv.*
first *adj., adv., n.*
   at first
fish *n.*
fit *v., adj.*
fix *v.*
fixed *adj.*
flag *n.*
flame *n.*
flash *v.*
flat *adj.*
flavor *n.*
flight *n.*

float *v.*
flood *n.*
floor *n.*
flour *n.*
flow *v.*
flower *n.*
fly *v.*
fold *v.*
follow *v.*
food *n.*
foot *n.*
football *n.*
for *prep.*
force *n., v.*
foreign *adj.*
forest *n.*
forever *adv.*
forget *v.*
forgive *v.*
fork *n.*
form *n., v.*
formal *adj.*
forward *adv.*
frame *n.*
free *adj., v., adv.*
freedom *n.*
freeze *v.*
fresh *adj.*
friend *n.*
friendly *adj.*
friendship *n.*
frighten *v.*
from *prep.*
front *n., adj.*
   in front
frozen *adj.*
fruit *n.*
fry *v.*
fuel *n.*
full *adj.*
fully *adv.*
fun *n., adj.*
funny *adj.*
fur *n.*
furniture *n.*
further *adj., adv.*
future *n., adj.*

G

gain *v.*
gallon *n.*
game *n.*
garbage *n.*
garden *n.*
gas *n.*
gate *n.*
general *adj.*
   in general
generally *adv.*

generous *adj.*
gentle *adj.*
gently *adv.*
gentleman *n.*
get *v.*
gift *n.*
girl *n.*
girlfriend *n.*
give *v.*
glass *n.*
glasses *n.*
global *adj.*
glove *n.*
go *v.*
goal *n.*
god *n.*
gold *n., adj.*
good *adj., n.*
goodbye *exclamation*
goods *n.*
govern *v.*
government *n.*
grade *n., v.*
grain *n.*
gram *n.*
grammar *n.*
grandchild *n.*
grandfather *n.*
grandmother *n.*
grandparent *n.*
grass *n.*
grateful *adj.*
gray *adj., n.*
great *adj.*
green *adj., n.*
groceries *n.*
ground *n.*
group *n.*
grow *v.*
growth *n.*
guard *n., v.*
guess *v.*
guest *n.*
guide *n.*
guilty *adj.*
gun *n.*

H

habit *n.*
hair *n.*
half *n., adj., pron., adv.*
hall *n.*
hammer *n.*
hand *n.*
handle *v., n.*
hang *v.*
happen *v.*
happiness *n.*
happy *adj.*

hard *adj., adv.*
hardly *adv.*
harm *n., v.*
harmful *adj.*
hat *n.*
hate *v., n.*
have *v.*
    have to *modal v.*
he *pron.*
head *n.*
health *n.*
healthy *adj.*
hear *v.*
heart *n.*
heat *n., v.*
heavy *adj.*
height *n.*
hello *exclamation*
help *v., n.*
helpful *adj.*
her *pron., adj.*
here *adv.*
hers *pron.*
herself *pron.*
hide *v.*
high *adj., adv.*
highly *adv.*
high school *n.*
highway *n.*
hill *n.*
him *pron.*
himself *pron.*
hire *v.*
his *adj., pron.*
history *n.*
hit *v., n.*
hold *v., n.*
hole *n.*
holiday *n.*
home *n., adv..*
honest *adj.*
hook *n.*
hope *v., n.*
horn *n.*
horse *n.*
hospital *n.*
hot *adj.*
hotel *n.*
hour *n.*
house *n.*
how *adv.*
however *adv.*
huge *adj.*
human *adj., n.*
humor *n.*
hungry *adj.*
hunt *v.*
hurry *v., n.*
hurt *v.*

husband *n.*

I
I *pron.*
ice *n.*
idea *n.*
identify *v.*
if *conj.*
ignore *v.*
illegal *adj.*
illegally *adv.*
illness *n.*
image *n.*
imagination *n.*
imagine *v.*
immediate *adj.*
immediately *adv.*
impatient *adj.*
importance *n.*
important *adj.*
impossible *adj.*
impress *v.*
impression *n.*
improve *v.*
improvement *n.*
in *prep., adv.*
inch *n.*
include *v.*
including *prep.*
increase *v., n.*
indeed *adv.*
independent *adj.*
individual *adj.*
industry *n.*
infection *n.*
influence *n.*
inform *v.*
informal *adj.*
information *n.*
injure *v.*
injury *n.*
insect *n.*
inside *prep., adv., n., adj.*
instead *adv., prep.*
instruction *n.*
instrument *n.*
insult *v., n.*
intelligent *adj.*
intend *v.*
intention *n.*
interest *n., v.*
interested *adj.*
interesting *adj.*
international *adj.*
Internet *n.*
interrupt *v.*
interview *n.*
into *prep.*
introduce *v.*

introduction *n.*
invent *v.*
investigate *v.*
invitation *n.*
invite *v.*
involve *v.*
iron *n.*
island *n.*
issue *n.*
it *pron.*
item *n.*
its *adj.*
itself *pron.*

J
jacket *n.*
jeans *n.*
jewelry *n.*
job *n.*
join *v.*
joke *n., v.*
judge *n., v.*
judgment (*also*
    judgement) *n.*
juice *n.*
jump *v.*
just *adv.*

K
keep *v.*
key *n.*
kick *v., n.*
kid *n., v.*
kill *v.*
kilogram (*also* kilo) *n.*
kilometer *n.*
kind *n., adj.*
kindness *n.*
king *n.*
kiss *v., n.*
kitchen *n.*
knee *n.*
knife *n.*
knock *v., n.*
knot *n.*
know *v.*
knowledge *n.*

L
lack *n.*
lady *n.*
lake *n.*
lamp *n.*
land *n., v.*
language *n.*
large *adj.*
last *adj., adv., n., v.*
late *adj., adv.*
later *adv.*

laugh *v.*
laundry *n.*
law *n.*
lawyer *n.*
lay *v.*
layer *n.*
lazy *adj.*
lead /lid/ *v.*
leader *n.*
leaf *n.*
lean *v.*
learn *v.*
least *adj., pron., adv.*
    at least
leather *n.*
leave *v.*
left *adj., adv., n.*
leg *n.*
legal *adj.*
legally *adv.*
lemon *n.*
lend *v.*
length *n.*
less *adj., pron., adv.*
lesson *n.*
let *v.*
letter *n.*
level *n.*
library *n.*
lid *n.*
lie *v., n.*
life *n.*
lift *v.*
light *n., adj., v.*
lightly *adv.*
like *prep., v., conj.*
likely *adj.*
limit *n., v.*
line *n.*
lip *n.*
liquid *n., adj.*
list *n., v.*
listen *v.*
liter *n.*
literature *n.*
little *adj., pron., adv.*
    a little
live /lɪv/ *v.*
living *adj.*
load *n., v.*
loan *n.*
local *adj.*
lock *v., n.*
lonely *adj.*
long *adj., adv.*
look *v., n.*
loose *adj.*
lose *v.*
loss *n.*

The Oxford 2000 List of Keywords

lost *adj.*
lot *pron., adv.*
   a lot (of)
   lots (of)
loud *adj.*
loudly *adv.*
love *n., v.*
low *adj., adv.*
luck *n.*
lucky *adj.*
lump *n.*
lunch *n.*

M

machine *n.*
magazine *n.*
magic *n., adj.*
mail *n., v.*
main *adj.*
mainly *adv.*
make *v.*
male *adj., n.*
man *n.*
manage *v.*
manager *n.*
many *adj., pron.*
map *n.*
mark *n., v.*
market *n.*
marriage *n.*
married *adj.*
marry *v.*
match *n., v.*
material *n.*
math *n.*
mathematics *n.*
matter *n., v.*
may *modal v.*
maybe *adv.*
me *pron.*
meal *n.*
mean *v.*
meaning *n.*
measure *v., n.*
measurement *n.*
meat *n.*
medical *adj.*
medicine *n.*
medium *adj.*
meet *v.*
meeting *n.*
melt *v.*
member *n.*
memory *n.*
mental *adj.*
mention *v.*
mess *n.*
message *n.*
messy *adj.*

metal *n.*
method *n.*
meter *n.*
middle *n., adj.*
midnight *n.*
might *modal v.*
mile *n.*
milk *n.*
mind *n., v.*
mine *pron.*
minute *n.*
mirror *n.*
Miss *n.*
miss *v.*
missing *adj.*
mistake *n.*
mix *v.*
mixture *n.*
model *n.*
modern *adj.*
mom *n.*
moment *n.*
money *n.*
month *n.*
mood *n.*
moon *n.*
moral *adj.*
morally *adv.*
more *adj., pron., adv.*
morning *n.*
most *adj., pron., adv.*
mostly *adv.*
mother *n.*
motorcycle *n.*
mountain *n.*
mouse *n.*
mouth *n.*
move *v., n.*
movement *n.*
movie *n.*
Mr. *abbr.*
Mrs. *abbr.*
Ms. *abbr.*
much *adj., pron., adv.*
mud *n.*
multiply *v.*
murder *n., v.*
muscle *n.*
museum *n.*
music *n.*
musical *adj.*
musician *n.*
must *modal v.*
my *adj.*
myself *pron.*
mysterious *adj.*

N

nail *n.*

name *n., v.*
narrow *adj.*
nation *n.*
national *adj.*
natural *adj.*
nature *n.*
navy *n.*
near *adj., adv., prep.*
nearby *adj., adv.*
nearly *adv.*
neat *adj.*
neatly *adv.*
necessary *adj.*
neck *n.*
need *v., n.*
needle *n.*
negative *adj.*
neighbor *n.*
neither *adj., pron., adv.*
nerve *n.*
nervous *adj.*
net *n.*
never *adv.*
new *adj.*
news *n.*
newspaper *n.*
next *adj., adv., n.*
nice *adj.*
night *n.*
no *exclamation, adj.*
nobody *pron.*
noise *n.*
noisy *adj.*
noisily *adv.*
none *pron.*
nonsense *n.*
no one *pron.*
nor *conj.*
normal *adj.*
normally *adv.*
north *n., adj., adv.*
northern *adj.*
nose *n.*
not *adv.*
note *n.*
nothing *pron.*
notice *v.*
novel *n.*
now *adv.*
nowhere *adv.*
nuclear *adj.*
number (*abbr.* No., no.) *n.*
nurse *n.*
nut *n.*

O

object *n.*
obtain *v.*
obvious *adj.*

occasion *n.*
occur *v.*
ocean *n.*
o'clock *adv.*
odd *adj.*
of *prep.*
off *adv., prep.*
offense *n.*
offer *v., n.*
office *n.*
officer *n.*
official *adj., n.*
officially *adv.*
often *adv.*
oh *exclamation*
oil *n.*
OK (*also* okay)
   exclamation, adj., adv.
old *adj.*
old-fashioned *adj.*
on *prep., adv.*
once *adv., conj.*
one *number, adj., pron.*
onion *n.*
only *adj., adv.*
onto *prep.*
open *adj., v..*
operate *v.*
operation *n.*
opinion *n.*
opportunity *n.*
opposite *adj., adv., n., prep.*
or *conj.*
orange *n., adj.*
order *n., v.*
ordinary *adj.*
organization *n.*
organize *v.*
organized *adj.*
original *adj., n.*
other *adj., pron.*
otherwise *adv.*
ought to *modal v.*
ounce *n.*
our *adj.*
ours *pron.*
ourselves *pron.*
out *adj., adv.*
out of *prep.*
outside *n., adj., prep., adv.*
oven *n.*
over *adv., prep.*
owe *v.*
own *adj., pron., v.*
owner *n.*

P

pack *v., n.*
package *n.*

page *n.*
pain *n.*
painful *adj.*
paint *n., v.*
painter *n.*
painting *n.*
pair *n.*
pale *adj.*
pan *n.*
pants *n.*
paper *n.*
parent *n.*
park *n., v.*
part *n.*
   take part (in)
particular *adj.*
particularly *adv.*
partly *adv.*
partner *n.*
party *n.*
pass *v.*
passage *n.*
passenger *n.*
passport *n.*
past *adj., n., prep., adv.*
path *n.*
patient *n., adj.*
pattern *n.*
pause *v.*
pay *v., n.*
payment *n.*
peace *n.*
peaceful *adj.*
pen *n.*
pencil *n.*
people *n.*
perfect *adj.*
perform *v.*
performance *n.*
perhaps *adv.*
period *n.*
permanent *adj.*
permission *n.*
person *n.*
personal *adj.*
personality *n.*
persuade *v.*
pet *n.*
phone *n.*
photo *n.*
photograph *n.*
phrase *n.*
physical *adj.*
physically *adv.*
piano *n.*
pick *v.*
   pick sth up
picture *n.*
piece *n.*

pig *n.*
pile *n.*
pilot *n.*
pin *n.*
pink *adj., n.*
pint *n.*
pipe *n.*
place *n., v.*
   take place
plain *adj.*
plan *n., v.*
plane *n.*
planet *n.*
plant *n., v.*
plastic *n.*
plate *n.*
play *v., n.*
player *n.*
pleasant *adj.*
please *exclamation, v.*
pleased *adj.*
pleasure *n.*
plenty *pron.*
pocket *n.*
poem *n.*
poetry *n.*
point *n., v.*
pointed *adj.*
poison *n., v.*
poisonous *adj.*
police *n.*
polite *adj.*
politely *adv.*
political *adj.*
politician *n.*
politics *n.*
pollution *n.*
pool *n.*
poor *adj.*
popular *adj.*
port *n.*
position *n.*
positive *adj.*
possibility *n.*
possible *adj.*
possibly *adv.*
post *n.*
pot *n.*
potato *n.*
pound *n.*
pour *v.*
powder *n.*
power *n.*
powerful *adj.*
practical *adj.*
practice *n., v.*
prayer *n.*
prefer *v.*
pregnant *adj.*

preparation *n.*
prepare *v.*
present *adj., n., v.*
president *n.*
press *n., v.*
pressure *n.*
pretend *v.*
pretty *adv., adj.*
prevent *v.*
previous *adj.*
price *n.*
priest *n.*
principal *n.*
print *v.*
priority *n.*
prison *n.*
prisoner *n.*
private *adj.*
prize *n.*
probable *adj.*
probably *adv.*
problem *n.*
process *n.*
produce *v.*
product *n.*
production *n.*
professional *adj.*
profit *n.*
program *n.*
progress *n.*
project *n.*
promise *v., n.*
pronunciation *n.*
proof *n.*
proper *adj.*
property *n.*
protect *v.*
protection *n.*
protest *n.*
proud *adj.*
prove *v.*
provide *v.*
public *adj., n.*
   publicly *adv.*
publish *v.*
pull *v.*
punish *v.*
punishment *n.*
pure *adj.*
purple *adj., n.*
purpose *n.*
   on purpose
push *v., n.*
put *v.*

Q
quality *n.*
quantity *n.*
quarter *n.*

queen *n.*
question *n., v.*
quick *adj.*
quickly *adv.*
quiet *adj.*
quietly *adv.*
quite *adv.*

R
race *n., v.*
radio *n.*
railroad *n.*
rain *n., v.*
raise *v.*
rare *adj.*
rarely *adv.*
rate *n.*
rather *adv.*
reach *v.*
reaction *n.*
read *v.*
ready *adj.*
real *adj.*
reality *n.*
realize *v.*
really *adv.*
reason *n.*
reasonable *adj.*
receive *v.*
recent *adj.*
recently *adv.*
recognize *v.*
recommend *v.*
record *n., v.*
recover *v.*
red *adj., n.*
reduce *v.*
refer to *v.*
refuse *v.*
region *n.*
regular *adj.*
regularly *adv.*
relation *n.*
relationship *n.*
relax *v.*
relaxed *adj.*
release *v.*
relevant *adj.*
relief *n.*
religion *n.*
religious *adj.*
rely *v.*
remain *v.*
remark *n.*
remember *v.*
remind *v.*
remove *v.*
rent *n., v.*
repair *v., n.*

The Oxford 2000 List of Keywords

repeat *v.*
replace *v.*
reply *n., v.*
report *v., n.*
reporter *n.*
represent *v.*
request *n., v.*
require *v.*
rescue *v.*
research *n., v.*
reservation *n.*
respect *n., v.*
responsibility *n.*
responsible *adj.*
rest *n., v.*
restaurant *n.*
result *n., v.*
return *v., n.*
rice *n.*
rich *adj.*
rid *v.: get rid of*
ride *v., n.*
right *adj., adv., n.*
ring *n., v.*
rise *n., v.*
risk *n., v.*
river *n.*
road *n.*
rob *v.*
rock *n.*
role *n.*
roll *n., v.*
romantic *adj.*
roof *n.*
room *n.*
root *n.*
rope *n.*
rough *adj.*
round *adj.*
route *n.*
row *n.*
royal *adj.*
rub *v.*
rubber *n.*
rude *adj.*
    rudely *adv.*
ruin *v.*
rule *n., v.*
run *v., n.*
rush *v.*

S
sad *adj.*
sadness *n.*
safe *adj.*
safely *adv.*
safety *n.*
sail *v.*
salad *n.*

sale *n.*
salt *n.*
same *adj., pron.*
sand *n.*
satisfaction *n.*
satisfied *adj.*
sauce *n.*
save *v.*
say *v.*
scale *n.*
scare *v.*
scared *adj.*
scary *adj.*
schedule *n.*
school *n.*
science *n.*
scientific *adj.*
scientist *n.*
scissors *n.*
score *n., v.*
scratch *v., n.*
screen *n.*
search *n., v.*
season *n.*
seat *n.*
second *adj., adv., n.*
secret *adj., n.*
secretary *n.*
secretly *adv.*
section *n.*
see *v.*
seed *n.*
seem *v.*
sell *v.*
send *v.*
senior *adj.*
sense *n.*
sensible *adj.*
sensitive *adj.*
sentence n.
separate *adj., v.*
separately *adv.*
series *n.*
serious *adj.*
serve *v.*
service *n.*
set *n., v.*
settle *v.*
several *adj., pron.*
sew *v.*
sex *n.*
sexual *adj.*
shade *n.*
shadow *n.*
shake *v.*
shame *n.*
shape *n., v.*
    shaped *adj.*
share *v., n.*

sharp *adj.*
she *pron.*
sheep *n.*
sheet *n.*
shelf *n.*
shell *n.*
shine *v.*
shiny *adj.*
ship *n.*
shirt *n.*
shock *n., v.*
shoe *n.*
shoot *v.*
shop *v.*
shopping *n.*
short *adj.*
shot *n.*
should *modal v.*
shoulder *n.*
shout *v., n.*
show *v., n.*
shower *n.*
shut *v.*
shy *adj.*
sick *adj.*
side *n.*
sight *n.*
sign *n., v.*
signal *n.*
silence *n.*
silly *adj.*
silver *n., adj.*
similar *adj.*
simple *adj.*
since *prep., conj., adv.*
sing *v.*
singer *n.*
single *adj.*
sink *v.*
sir *n.*
sister *n.*
sit *v.*
situation *n.*
size *n.*
skill *n.*
skin *n.*
skirt *n.*
sky *n.*
sleep *v., n.*
sleeve *n.*
slice *n.*
slide *v.*
slightly *adv.*
slip *v.*
slow *adj.*
slowly *adv.*
small *adj.*
smell *v., n.*
smile *v., n.*

smoke *n., v.*
smooth *adj.*
    smoothly *adv.*
snake *n.*
snow *n., v.*
so *adv., conj.*
soap *n.*
social *adj.*
society *n.*
sock *n.*
soft *adj.*
soil *n.*
soldier *n.*
solid *adj., n.*
solution *n.*
solve *v.*
some *adj., pron.*
somebody *pron.*
somehow *adv.*
someone *pron.*
something *pron.*
sometimes *adv.*
somewhere *adv.*
son *n.*
song *n.*
soon *adv.*
    as soon as
sore *adj.*
sorry *adj.*
sort *n., v.*
sound *n., v.*
soup *n.*
south *n., adj., adv.*
southern *adj.*
space *n.*
speak *v.*
speaker *n.*
special *adj.*
speech *n.*
speed *n.*
spell *v.*
spend *v.*
spice *n.*
spider *n.*
spirit *n.*
spoil *v.*
spoon *n.*
sport *n.*
spot *n.*
spread *v.*
spring *n.*
square *adj., n.*
stage *n.*
stair *n.*
stamp *n.*
stand *v., n.*
standard *n., adj.*
star *n.*
stare *v.*

start *v., n.*
state *n., v.*
statement *n.*
station *n.*
stay *v.*
steady *adj.*
steal *v.*
steam *n.*
step *n., v.*
stick *v., n.*
sticky *adj.*
still *adv., adj.*
stomach *n.*
stone *n.*
stop *v., n.*
store *n., v.*
storm *n.*
story *n.*
stove *n.*
straight *adv., adj.*
strange *adj.*
street *n.*
strength *n.*
stress *n.*
stretch *v.*
strict *adj.*
string *n.*
strong *adj.*
strongly *adv.*
structure *n.*
struggle *v., n.*
student *n.*
study *n., v.*
stuff *n.*
stupid *adj.*
style *n.*
subject *n.*
substance *n.*
succeed *v.*
success *n.*
successful *adj.*
successfully *adv.*
such *adj.*
   such as
suck *v.*
sudden *adj.*
suddenly *adv.*
suffer *v.*
sugar *n.*
suggest *v.*
suggestion *n.*
suit *n.*
suitable *adj.*
sum *n.*
summer *n.*
sun *n.*
supply *n.*
support *n., v.*
suppose *v.*

sure *adj., adv.*
surface *n.*
surprise *n., v.*
surprised *adj.*
surround *v.*
survive *v.*
swallow *v.*
swear *v.*
sweat *n., v.*
sweet *adj.*
swim *v.*
switch *n., v.*
symbol *n.*
system *n.*

T
table *n.*
tail *n.*
take *v.*
talk *v., n.*
tall *adj.*
tape *n.*
task *n.*
taste *n., v.*
tax *n.*
tea *n.*
teach *v.*
teacher *n.*
team *n.*
tear /tɛr/ *v.*
tear /tɪr/ *n.*
technical *adj.*
technology *n.*
telephone *n.*
television *n.*
tell *v.*
temperature *n.*
temporary *adj.*
tend *v.*
terrible *adj.*
test *n., v.*
text *n.*
than *prep., conj.*
thank *v.*
thanks *n.*
thank you *n.*
that *adj., pron., conj.*
the *definite article*
theater *n.*
their *adj.*
theirs *pron.*
them *pron.*
themselves *pron.*
then *adv.*
there *adv.*
therefore *adv.*
they *pron.*
thick *adj.*
thin *adj.*

thing *n.*
think *v.*
thirsty *adj.*
this *adj., pron.*
though *conj., adv.*
thought *n.*
thread *n.*
threat *n.*
threaten *v.*
throat *n.*
through *prep., adv.*
throw *v.*
thumb *n.*
ticket *n.*
tie *v., n.*
tight *adj., adv.*
time *n.*
tire *n.*
tired *adj.*
title *n.*
to *prep., infinitive marker*
today *adv., n.*
toe *n.*
together *adv.*
toilet *n.*
tomato *n.*
tomorrow *adv., n.*
tongue *n.*
tonight *adv., n.*
too *adv.*
tool *n.*
tooth *n.*
top *n., adj.*
topic *n.*
total *adj., n.*
totally *adv.*
touch *v., n.*
tour *n.*
tourist *n.*
toward *prep.*
towel *n.*
town *n.*
toy *n.*
track *n.*
tradition *n.*
traffic *n.*
train *n., v.*
training *n.*
translate *v.*
transparent *adj.*
transportation *n.*
trash *n.*
travel *v., n.*
treat *v.*
treatment *n.*
tree *n.*
trial *n.*
trick *n.*
trip *n., v.*

trouble *n.*
truck *n.*
true *adj.*
trust *n., v.*
truth *n.*
try *v.*
tube *n.*
tune *n.*
tunnel *n.*
turn *v., n.*
TV *n.*
twice *adv.*
twist *v.*
type *n., v.*
typical *adj.*

U
ugly *adj.*
unable *adj.*
uncle *n.*
uncomfortable *adj.*
unconscious *adj.*
under *prep., adv.*
underground *adj., adv.*
understand *v.*
underwater *adj., adv.*
underwear *n.*
unemployment *n.*
unexpected *adj.*
unexpectedly *adv.*
unfair *adj.*
unfortunately *adv.*
unfriendly *adj.*
unhappy *adj.*
uniform *n.*
union *n.*
unit *n.*
universe *n.*
university *n.*
unkind *adj.*
unknown *adj.*
unless *conj.*
unlikely *adj.*
unlucky *adj.*
unpleasant *adj.*
until *conj., prep.*
unusual *adj.*
up *adv., prep.*
upper *adj.*
upset *v., adj.*
upstairs *adv., adj.*
upward *adv.*
urgent *adj.*
us *pron.*
use *v., n.*
used *adj.*
used to *modal v.*
useful *adj.*
user *n.*

The Oxford 2000 List of Keywords

usual *adj.*
usually *adv.*

V

vacation *n.*
valley *n.*
valuable *adj.*
value *n.*
variety *n.*
various *adj.*
vary *v.*
vegetable *n.*
vehicle *n.*
very *adv.*
video *n.*
view *n.*
violence *n.*
violent *adj.*
virtually *adv.*
visit *v., n.*
visitor *n.*
voice *n.*
volume *n.*
vote *n., v.*

W

wait *v.*
wake (up) *v.*
walk *v., n.*
wall *n.*
want *v.*
war *n.*
warm *adj., v.*
warn *v.*
wash *v.*
waste *v., n., adj.*
watch *v., n.*
water *n.*
wave *n., v.*
way *n.*
we *pron.*
weak *adj.*
weakness *n.*
weapon *n.*
wear *v.*
weather *n.*
website *n.*
wedding *n.*
week *n.*
weekend *n.*
weigh *v.*
weight *n.*
welcome *v.*
well *adv., adj., exclamation*
  as well (as)
west *n., adj., adv.*
western *adj.*
wet *adj.*
what *pron., adj.*

whatever *adj., pron., adv.*
wheel *n.*
when *adv., conj.*
whenever *conj.*
where *adv., conj.*
wherever *conj.*
whether *conj.*
which *pron., adj.*
while *conj., n.*
white *adj., n.*
who *pron.*
whoever *pron.*
whole *adj., n.*
whose *adj., pron.*
why *adv.*
wide *adj.*
wife *n.*
wild *adj.*
will *modal v., n.*
win *v.*
wind /wɪnd/ *n.*
window *n.*
wine *n.*
wing *n.*
winner *n.*
winter *n.*
wire *n.*
wish *v., n.*
with *prep.*
within *prep.*
without *prep.*
woman *n.*
wonder *v.*
wonderful *adj.*
wood *n.*
wooden *adj.*
wool *n.*
word *n.*
work *v., n.*
worker *n.*
world *n.*
worried *adj.*
worry *v.*
worse *adj., adv.*
worst *adj., adv., n.*
worth *adj.*
would *modal v.*
wrap *v.*
wrist *n.*
write *v.*
writer *n.*
writing *n.*
wrong *adj., adv.*

Y

yard *n.*
year *n.*
yellow *adj., n.*
yes *exclamation*

yesterday *adv., n.*
yet *adv.*
you *pron.*
young *adj.*
your *adj.*
yours *pron.*
yourself *pron.*
youth *n.*